D0193972

Off Balance

Off Balance

Getting Beyond
the Work-Life Balance Myth
to
Personal and Professional Satisfaction

———————

Matthew Kelly

BEACON

OFF BALANCE

Copyright © 2015 by Beacon Publishing

First published by Hudson Street Press, a member of Penguin Group (USA) Inc.

B
E
A
C
O
N

LIBRARY OF CONGRESS CATALOGING-IN-PUBLICATION DATA

Kelly, Matthew.
Off balance : getting beyond the work-life balance myth to personal and professional satisfaction / Matthew Kelly.
    p. cm.
ISBN 978-1-942611-33-2. Work-life balance.   2. Job satisfaction.   3. Quality of work life.   4. Quality of life.   I. Title.
HF5549.5.J63K44 2011
650.1—dc22   2011007226

Without limiting the rights under copyright reserved above, no part of this publication may be reproduced, stored in or introduced into a retrieval system, or transmitted, in any form, or by any means (electronic, mechanical, photocopying, recording, or otherwise), without the prior written permission of both the copyright owner and the above publisher of this book.

Printed in the United States of America

Designed by Level C

10 9 8 7 6 5 4 3 2 1

This book is printed on acid-free paper.   ∞

Contents

Introduction

The Dilemma

One of the major issues plaguing human potential in the corporate world today is work-life balance. The term was first introduced twenty years ago and is likely to go down as one of the great corporate blunders of our time. While the work-life balance discussion was introduced with the very best of intentions—namely, to help people deal with the mounting pressures surrounding both personal and professional life in the modern world—in many ways the idea never had a chance because the term itself was fatally flawed.

The future of an organization and the potential of its employees are intertwined; their destinies are linked. An organization can only become the-best-version-of-itself to the extent that the people who drive that organization are becoming better-versions-of-themselves. To the extent that a CEO, an executive team, and a group of managers and employees explore their potential as individuals, so too will an organization explore its potential.

Think about it. Is your work part of your life? Of course it is. But when companies started asking employees if they had work-life balance, they separated work from the rest of an employee's life. They were essentially saying, "Your work isn't part of your life!" Now, the average person spends more time working each day than doing anything else. So it should be no surprise that employees didn't respond too favorably to the work-life balance questions on employee satisfaction surveys and began to demand more and more work-life balance. This always equates to working less. I am not aware of a single employee who has approached his manager and said, "I don't have work-life balance. I really feel that in order to solve the problem I need to work more."

The work-life balance conversation that has dominated the corporate landscape for almost two decades implies that work and life are separate. In this way, we set work and life against each other, and the thought that follows is that you are either working too much and living too little or vice versa. The term itself diminishes our ability to make the case that work can be a richly rewarding part of a person's life and should in many ways be personal.

You cannot separate the personal and professional aspects of an individual's life. You can consider them separately to gain insight, but the practical separation of the two is impossible.

They are intimately linked. If I come to work today and my wife is sick at home, I will be a little distracted and disengaged. If I wasn't, I would not be a good husband, and if that is the case, I am probably also not as good an employee as I could be. In the same way, if I successfully complete a great project at work today, I will be filled with a very positive energy and I will take that buoyant energy home to my wife and family. It is impossible to completely separate the personal from the professional; they are deeply intertwined.

There are some events in our lives that are personal and others that are professional. But you do not have two lives, one personal and one professional. You have one life that has personal and professional aspects, and these aspects have an incredible influence on each other. Having a baby is incredibly personal, but it affects your professional life. The death of a loved one is deeply personal, but it affects your professional life. Meeting your quarterly targets is overwhelmingly a professional matter, but it affects your personal life. Attracting a new customer or team member to your company is entirely professional, but the quest to do so will affect your personal life.

After twenty years of the work-life balance conversation, people are tired and frustrated. They have tried repeatedly to acquire the illusive work-life balance and have failed. Companies have spent tens of millions of dollars on programs, many employees have made valiant efforts to establish some sense of work-life balance, and we don't seem to have shifted the dial.

In fact, according to *Newsweek* 70 percent of employees say they have less work-life balance today than they did ten years ago. Realizing their missteps, some companies have renamed work-life balance as "work-life effectiveness." But the essential dilemma remains: corporations have failed to teach employees to effectively manage the various demands of personal and professional life, and employees have not found another way to learn them.

Having examined the issue extensively, I have come to the conclusion that people don't really need or want balance. As an idea, balance sounds desirable, but before we started discussing work-life balance I am not sure there was any great epidemic of people lying awake at night thinking to themselves, "I need balance. I want balance. Balance is the solution to all my problems." And even today, when people say they want more work-life balance, if you delve a little further and get people talking about what that balance looks like, you will discover that what they want has very little to do with balance.

So, what is it that people need and want? People need and want a satisfying experience of life. Over the past three years I have asked more than ten thousand respondents, "If you had to choose between balance and satisfaction, which would you choose?" Not a single respondent chose balance over satisfaction. People want to live deeply satisfying lives both personally and professionally. They want to know that both are possible at the same time. They want to be told that they don't have to sacrifice their personal priorities on the altar of corporate America in order to have a satisfying career. People want personal and professional satisfaction (PPS).

Here again, in the quest for satisfaction, we discover that the personal and the professional are deeply linked. It doesn't matter how satisfying the personal aspects of your life are, if you are miserable at work, that misery will spill over and create dissatisfaction that affects you both personally and professionally.

So where do we go from here? The answer was always right before us. The forum in which the work-life balance discussion emerged was the employee satisfaction survey. It was always about satisfaction. That's what people yearn for. Sometimes that satisfaction comes from working an eighty-hour week, and sometimes it comes from lying on a beach for a few days completely unplugged from the world of work. But most of the time, living a life that is deeply satisfying requires a strategy, daily attention, self-awareness, and discipline.

Our work-life balance efforts always lacked a comprehensive strategy. We threw a bunch of ideas and tools at people and expected them to formulate a practical strategy. The results now clearly demonstrate that most people are incapable of doing that. Interestingly, we often do the same thing in the area of professional work. We throw a bunch of ideas and tools at people and expect them to come up with a feasible strategy and then to work the strategy responsibly. We assume people are capable of this—many are not. We assume that people will approach their work strategically—most do not. Whether it is creating personal and professional satisfaction or delivering quarterly targets, people need a system.

Systems drive behaviors. Certain behaviors lead to certain outcomes. If you know what outcome you desire, the next step is to identify what type of behaviors will produce that outcome. Then all that is left is to build a system that supports and encourages those behaviors.

There are many things a company can and should do to help its employees pursue satisfying lives. First and foremost is to provide a comprehensive system that drives personal and professional satisfaction. It makes sense for a company to do these things purely from a position of self-interest. Employees who approach their lives strategically are more likely to approach their work strategically. Satisfied employees are more productive, they are more creative, and they provide superior customer service. But the primary responsibility for creating a satisfying life rests with the individual.

The promise of this book is to help you design and build a more satisfying life in both the personal and professional arenas. We will do this together by approaching our lives with the strategy and rigor with which the very best companies in the world approach business. The result is a personalized system that you will be able to apply to your life, year after year, to drive higher levels of satisfaction. If you are faithful to the system, I promise you this book will change your life.

Off Balance

Prologue

The Fisherman

Once upon a time there was an investment banker. He lived in New York City, was phenomenally successful, and made a ton of money. But his life was busy, noisy, and very stressful.

So, once a year, he would leave the city and go down to a small coastal village in Mexico. For two weeks he would rest, relax, and allow himself to be rejuvenated.

One day he was standing on the pier just before lunch, looking out to sea, when he noticed a small fishing boat coming in to dock. He thought this was a little strange because most of the fishermen stayed out late into the afternoon so they could catch as many fish as possible before coming in and preparing the fish for market.

Curiosity overcame him. So he walked over to where the fishing boat was about to dock. Looking into the boat, he saw just one fisherman and several large yellowfin tuna.

"How long did it take you to catch those fish?" he said to the fisherman.

"Not very long," the fisherman replied with a smile.

"Is there something wrong with your boat?" the American asked.

"Oh, no," the fisherman said. "In thirteen years I have never had a problem with the boat."

The American was a little perplexed, so he asked the fisherman, "Why don't you stay out there longer and catch more fish?"

The fisherman smiled again and said, "This is plenty here for my family right now. Some of the fish we can eat, and the others we can sell or trade for the other things we need."

"But it's not even lunchtime. What do you do with the rest of your time?"

"In the morning," the fisherman explained, "I like to sleep late. When I wake I fish a little, mostly just for the pleasure of fishing. In the afternoon I play with my children and take siesta with my wife. In the evenings I have dinner with my family. And then, when my children are sleeping, I stroll into the village, where I sip wine and play guitar with my friends."

The American scoffed and said, "I'm a Harvard MBA and I can help you."

The fisherman was a little skeptical, but nonetheless he obliged and asked, "How?"

"You should fish longer every day," the American counseled,

"late into the afternoon. This way you will catch more fish and make more money, and you can buy a bigger boat. With the bigger boat you will catch even more fish and make even more money, and then you can buy another boat and hire another man to work the second boat."

"But what then?" the fisherman inquired.

"Oh, we are just getting started! With two boats you'll catch even more fish and make even more money, and before you know it, you'll have a whole fleet of boats and every man in the village looking for work will come to you."

"But what then?" the fisherman asked.

"Before too long, you can cut out the middleman, sell your fish direct to the cannery, and make more money. As your fleet of boats continues to expand, you can build your own cannery. And before you know it, you'll be able to leave this small coastal village, move to Mexico City, and manage your expanding enterprise."

"But what then?" the fisherman persisted.

"Well, then you can begin to ship your fish to different parts of the world. Down into Asia and Australia and up into North America. And as demand grows for your fish, you can leave Mexico City, move to Los Angeles, open a distribution plant there, and begin to ship your fish to Europe and every corner of the globe."

"But what then?" the fisherman asked again.

The American continued, "By then your business will be

one of the great ventures of the industry. You can move to New York City and manage your empire from the epicenter of the business world."

"How long will all this take?" the fisherman asked.

"Twenty-five, maybe thirty years," the banker explained.

"But what will I do then?" the fisherman asked.

The American's eyes lit up like a Christmas tree. "That's the best part," he said. "When the time is just right, you can go down to Wall Street, list your business as a public company, offer an IPO, and make millions and millions of dollars."

"Millions?" the fisherman asked.

"More money than you ever dreamed you could earn in ten lifetimes," the American explained.

"But what then?" the fisherman asked.

The American didn't know what to say. He had reached his climax. He was stumped. But then a thought crossed his mind and triggered an idea, and he turned once more to the fisherman and spoke.

"Well, then you could move to a small coastal village. . . . You could sleep late. . . . You could fish just for the pleasure of fishing. . . . In the afternoons you could take siesta with your wife. . . . In the evenings you could have dinner with your family . . . and then you could stroll into the village and sip wine and play guitar with your friends. . . ."

1

The Best Way to Live

If I told you that *you* could have the life of the fisherman, would you believe me? Perhaps you would, perhaps you wouldn't, and perhaps you would like to but would doubt me nonetheless. Maybe you would think it a ridiculous proposition and dismiss it immediately as nonsense. Or maybe you would become curious about the possibilities. Take a moment to think about it. Is it possible that you could have the life of the fisherman in the story?

The answer is yes. I am confident that you could have the fisherman's life if you really wanted it. But I don't think you really want it. You might enjoy it for two or three weeks, but that's a vacation, and vacations are not life. Then again, maybe you don't really want the life you have right now, so you figure the fisherman's life has to be better. That's a dangerous assumption, but at least it shines a light on your dissatisfaction—and from time to time it is good to get in touch with our dissatisfaction.

The Life You Really Want

When was the last time you sat down and really thought about it? A couple of years ago I went for my annual physical. I knew I could stand to lose a few pounds, but I felt perfectly healthy. A few hours later I was at my local hospital having a variety of scans, and the next morning my doctor was telling me I had cancer.

I looked healthy. I felt healthy. But I had cancer. I was thirty-five years old and I remember driving home from the doctor's office wondering . . . "Is this real? What does this really mean? How serious is this? Are the doctors telling me the whole story or trying to keep me in good spirits?"

Getting cancer turned out to be one of the best things that ever happened to me. You see, even though I consider myself a fairly introspective person and spend a lot of time pondering life's big questions, life was quickly and unconsciously getting away from me. Both personally and professionally I was coasting.

Over the next few months, throughout the process of surgery and treatments, I began to really think about the life I truly wanted to live. I quickly realized that I had been dating an incredible woman for four years and that it was time to embrace a life with her. I also realized that my work needed to change, not so much what I did as how I did it. Mostly I came to the realization that I had not been approaching my life very strategically. Subconsciously or, worse than that, unconsciously, I was approaching life with a "let's see what happens" attitude. This is a wonderful, childlike attitude, but when we are at our best we mix it with an equal portion of let's see what we can make happen.

Let's see what we can make happen. Not necessarily with your latest project at work, but with your life. Let's explore what is possible. Not in relation to your newest client, but when it comes to your marriage and family, your hobbies and interests, your passions and dreams.

So, let's start to think about the life you really want. I find the best way to do this is to ponder a few questions. You may choose to read straight through these questions and straight through to the end of the chapter, and that's fine. But I would encourage you to come back to these questions at different times in the coming days and weeks and spend a little time pondering each. It is my hope that they will help you explore what is possible.

1. What do you like about your life as it is today?

2. What don't you like about your life as it is today?

3. Do you feel trapped by any of the things that you don't like about your life today?

4. If you went to the doctor next week and he told you that you were dying and had one year to live, what would you do for the next year?

5. If you inherited $10 billion, what would you do with the rest of your life, and what would you do with the money?

6. What is holding you back from the life you really want?

7. If you could change three things about your life, what would they be?

It is too easy to let another week, month, year slip by without really thinking about the life we want to live. It is too easy to just let life happen to us. We don't sit down often enough and think about how we are living. We continue to spend more time planning our annual vacations than we spend planning our lives. This has to change if we are to enjoy immense satisfaction personally and professionally. You can stumble into a moderately satisfying life, but to sustain and increase that satisfaction requires a strategic approach and some real work. The promise of this book is that you can be the architect of a life that is both personally and professionally satisfying. But in order to design and build such a life for yourself, you will need to approach this task with the rigor and commitment the best companies in the world use to approach the development of a new product.

Designing a new life is same as making a new product!

There are many different ways you could live your life. Your talents, personality, and relationships make many lives possible. There are many paths you can choose to follow both personally and professionally. You don't have to settle for the life you stumbled into.

Every Life Has a Cost

The story about the fisherman and his life is a beautiful story, but a lot has been left out. The fisherman's life comes at a cost. Every life comes at a cost. Your life and mine come at a cost. Every choice we make eliminates other options, and those other options are part of the cost involved in the life we choose to live. The fisherman's life comes at a cost that I very much doubt you are willing to pay. I know I am not. That doesn't make us weak people. I suspect the reason why we are not willing to pay the price is because when all the cards are on the table, we don't really want the fisherman's life. So, let's take a closer look at the fisherman's life.

The fisherman doesn't have electricity, a phone, or access to the Internet. He doesn't own a single consumer product, doesn't have a 401(k) plan, and has no heating or air-conditioning. He has never been to a dentist and has no health plan; he has no bank account, never eats out at restaurants, and has no education beyond the fourth grade. He doesn't have a car, he has no television, and his wife makes most of his clothes. He has never traveled the world and is never likely to. In fact, he has never even been to Mexico City.

I assure you, you could have his life. The fisherman's lifestyle costs him less than $125 a month. To put that into perspective, if you invested $30,000 and received an annual return of 5 percent ($1,500), you could support the fisherman's lifestyle . . . even if you never caught a fish. But the bigger questions are, Do you really want his life? Would it be good for you? Would that life engage your talents and abilities in meaningful ways? Would you be satisfied? Furthermore, if you went home tonight and told your spouse that you wanted to start a new life, abandon the so-called rat race and model your new life on that of the fisherman in the story, how would he or she respond? If you have children, how would they feel about it?

If you really want the life of the fisherman, and you have $30,000 in the bank, or $30,000 worth of equity in your home, or $45,000 in your 401(k) (the government is going to want tax and penalties), please go off and get that life. If you don't have the $30,000 and you are willing to risk what you do have on your fishing ability, please go off and pursue that life. If you don't have the $30,000 and you are not willing to risk it all on your ability to fish, then please get busy earning and saving the $30,000 so that you can go off and pursue the life that you think is going to bring you satisfaction.

But I really don't think you want the life of the fisherman.

You probably wouldn't mind something halfway between the life you have today and the life of the fisherman. At least that's what most of us probably tell ourselves, because it is a measured response. Truth is, it is too early to tell. You may be closer than you think to the life you really want or you may be much further away than most. Discovering what will lead to the most satisfying life for you is what this book is about.

The story of the fisherman makes us stop and reflect upon the life we are living. It shines a light on the dissatisfaction in our lives, and while we may want a life a little more like the fisherman's life, the real question is, <u>what are we willing to do—and to give up</u>—in order to have it? The life you desire is there for the taking, but it comes at a cost. Life, like business, hinges on the successful allocation of scarce resources.

Get in Touch with Your Dissatisfaction

What the story of the fisherman really does is put us in touch with our dissatisfaction. We all have dissatisfaction, and getting in touch with it is a good thing. Identifying aspects of personal and professional dissatisfaction is critical, and if the work-life balance conversation has done anything it has certainly helped people to get in touch with their dissatisfaction. But once we are in touch with it, we usually tell ourselves that it is unavoidable or that radical changes would be required to improve our lives in any meaningful way. More often than not we tend to fantasize about some impossible version of the fisherman's life as the solution to our dissatisfaction, but do nothing about it.

You can do something about your dissatisfaction, and you would be surprised at how the simple process outlined in this book, consistently applied to your life, can transform a drowning sense of dissatisfaction into an incredible joy for life.

Living a more satisfying life is possible. Experiencing a deep sense of satisfaction both personally and professionally is possible—at the same time. You do not have to sacrifice personal satisfaction to have professional satisfaction—or vice versa.

You could have the life of the fisherman, and if that is what you really want, this book will help you to get it. But I'll say it again: I don't think you really want it. So, for you, this book will help you get in touch with your dissatisfaction, personally and professionally. It will also help you identify what matters most to you. It will help you design a life that aligns your daily activities with your values and priorities so that you can live a deeply satisfying life both personally and professionally. And that life will be even better than the fisherman's life—for you.

What we admire about the fisherman's life is the satisfaction it seems to bring him. We all yearn for that satisfaction.

How Is the Best Way to Live?

Every great civilization since the beginning of time has con-
cerned itself with a single question: how is the best way to live?
This is the primary question that the great philosophers of every
age have grappled with. It is the question every culture, country, generation, and individual consciously or unconsciously
wrestles with. It is also the question that the whole work-life
balance conversation of the past twenty years has been centered
upon. But most important, it is a question you and I grapple
with in a deeply personal way.

The rigor with which a person or culture approaches this
single question is very telling. It is of disturbing importance to
note that the present culture has virtually no interest in pursuing this question. We seem more interested in how we want to
live than we are in discovering the best way to live. Likewise,
we are much more interested in developing self-expression than
we are in developing selves that are worth expressing. Personal
preference has triumphed over the pursuit of excellence. We
want what we want, and we feel entitled to what we want.

The problem with all this is that getting what we want is certainly not work-life balance, and getting what we want almost
never leads to personal and professional satisfaction. The reason
is that very few people have the requisite self-knowledge to
want the right things. As we grow and gain this self-knowledge
we begin to want what we need because we discover that the

fulfillment of our legitimate needs is more likely to lead to lasting happiness in a changing world than the reckless pursuit of whimsical desires.

The desire to get what we want is usually tied much more to a pleasure principle than it is to any lasting satisfaction. Too often pleasure and satisfaction are confused. The very reason Mick Jagger "can't get no satisfaction" is that he has confused pleasure with satisfaction. Many people approach the work-life balance quest in the same way.

The fundamental difference between pleasure and satisfaction is that pleasure cannot be sustained beyond the activity producing it. When we eat we feel pleasure; when we stop eating the pleasure stops. That's why we don't stop eating. We're not hungry. In fact, 75 percent of the time when we are eating we are not hungry—but we love the pleasure of eating.

Satisfaction is very different. Consider this example. You come home from work and it is your day to work out. You don't feel like exercising and would rather collapse in front of the television, but you force yourself to work out. Interestingly, whenever we get done working out we are always glad we did—even if we had to force ourselves. That's satisfaction. Satisfaction can be sustained beyond the activity producing it. The people, places, things, and activities that have brought satisfaction to my life continue to satisfy me, while those that bring only pleasure to my life leave me with an unquenchable yearning for more of the same. Addiction is wanting more and more of something that brings less and less satisfaction. In many ways we have become addicted to pleasure, to getting what we want, and the cost is always genuine satisfaction. It is a mistake to think that pleasure and satisfaction go hand in hand. I can look back on projects that challenged me to my very core, some of which involved real misery, and feel genuinely satisfied. This satisfaction is much more important than enjoying our work—though combining both is optimal. But if I have to choose between enjoying my work and gaining real satisfaction from my work, I will choose satisfaction. In fact, I suspect there are a great many things that we would set aside if we had to choose between them and a deep and abiding satisfaction.

Outside the paradigm in which we want what we need and what is best for us, getting what we want never leads to the satisfaction we thought it would. Every one of us has experienced the letdown of accomplishing something or obtaining something and then realizing it to be empty and hollow, devoid of the satisfaction we thought it would be brimming with.

The work-life balance discussion was corporate America's attempt to answer the timeless question "How is the best way to live?" But I am not sure the corporate world is qualified to answer it. I don't mean that as a criticism in any way. A corporation cannot answer the question because in some ways the answer is different for everyone. Besides, surely each of us is responsible for asking and answering the question ourselves.

The Three Philosophies of Our Age

Everybody has a philosophy; whether or not we are able to articulate it in conversation or in writing is irrelevant, because we articulate it with our words and actions on a daily basis. Our present culture idolizes three practical philosophies that are eating away at the very fabric of our workforce and culture, our relationships, and our lives.

The first of these practical philosophies is individualism. When most people today are faced with a decision, the question that seems to dominate their inner dialogue is, "What's in it for me?" This question is the creed of individualism, which is based on an all-consuming concern for self. In the present climate, the most dominant trend governing the decision-making process is individualism.

Have you ever tried to work with a team where all its members were rugged individualists? Have you ever tried to manage an individualist?

No community, whether it is as small as a team or as large as a nation, can grow strong with this attitude. Individualism always weakens the community and causes the whole to suffer. In every instance it is a cancerous growth.

The fruits of individualism are no secret to any of us: greed, selfishness, and exploitation. What would become of a family, a team, or a nation in which each member adopted individualism as his or her own personal philosophy? Over time it would grow apart and fall apart.

This naked individualism is only furthered by the present generation's assertion that pleasure is the supreme good. This assertion unmasks hedonism as the second philosophical mark of our age. Hedonism is the philosophy that emphasizes pleasure as the ultimate goal of life. The motto, the creed, the catch cry of the hedonist is, "If it feels good, do it!"

Have you ever tried to work with a team in which everyone wanted to do only what was enjoyable?

Under the guise of a supposedly newfound freedom, this ancient impostor has seduced and deceived present generations. This is the great paradox regarding the philosophical marks of our age. The people who promote them represent them as new and different, but if we undress these philosophies we quickly discover that the present cultural environment is based on failed ideologies of the past. We mistakenly believe that these philosophies are new and different. But if we scratch just beneath the surface and look a little deeper, we will discover that the cultures that first employed these philosophies, or have since adopted them, can all trace their decline to them.

Whenever hedonism emerged as a dominant practical philosophy in other cultures and subcultures, it produced men and women who were lazy, lustful, and gluttonous. Furthermore, hedonism has been a contributing factor to the demise of every culture and subculture in which it has figured significantly. The Roman Empire is a perfect example.

Hedonism is not an expression of freedom; it is a passport to enslavement by a thousand cravings and addictions. And in the end it produces not pleasure but despair.

The third philosophical mark of our age perfectly complements the greed of individualism and the lust of hedonism in the demise of human character. Accompanying these other modern creeds—whose central tenets are "What's in it for me?" and "If it feels good, do it!"—is the creed of minimalism. The minimalist is always asking, "What is the least I can do?"

A minimalist is always seeking to exert the minimum effort and receive the maximum reward. Consciously or subconsciously, people everywhere seem to be asking, "What is the least I can do and still keep my job? What is the least I can do and still get reasonable grades in school? What is the least I can do and still keep my marriage alive? What is the least I can do and still stay physically fit? What is the least I can do . . . ?"

Minimalism is the enemy of excellence and the father of mediocrity. It is one of the greatest philosophical diseases of our age. Minimalism has infected every aspect of our lives and society and, tragically, it is also one of the philosophical diseases that is eating away at the corporate culture.

It is within the philosophical realms of individualism, hedonism, and minimalism that most people make the majority of their decisions every day. It is therefore not difficult to see that managing people is becoming increasingly difficult. And individualism, hedonism, and minimalism all lead to decreasing levels of satisfaction in a person's life. With all this in mind, we shouldn't be surprised that most people are not able to design a sustainable work-life balance framework for themselves.

Any community that adopts these philosophies, whether that community is a team, a family, a company, or a nation, does so at its own peril. A philosophy is a way of life. Individualism, hedonism, and minimalism will destroy every individual and community that practices them. They are ultimately self-destructive philosophies that destroy body, heart, mind, and soul.

The crisis of the modern world is a crisis of ideas. Ideas shape our lives and the world. Thought determines action. It would not be too soon for us to learn that ideas have very real consequences.

These philosophies are little more than lazy attempts to answer the question "How is the best way to live?"

The Random List

Many people, perhaps most, have some random ideas about the best way to live. These random ideas rarely reflect any comprehensive strategy. If you search Google for "the best way to live," you come up with all sorts of weird and wonderful perspectives. I found one great list, at Bestuff.com, which invites people to vote on the items. Here is the list, in order of most to least votes.

The best way to live . . .

- With an open mind
- Doing what you want, when you want, and not having to answer to anyone
- Never losing sight of what's really important
- Being an individual
- Living instead of existing
- Laughing at yourself
- Writing stories
- Dressing uniquely
- Not giving up hope
- Positive thinking
- Lying in grass, looking for shapes in the clouds
- Living for today but planning for tomorrow
- Believing in the ones who deserve it the most
- Getting lost in music

- Being spontaneous

- Being strange

- Dancing

- Being alone

- Living a bold life

- Vanity

- Unending curiosity

- Living on a farm

- Living it up

I found it interesting that, of the thousands of people who had voted, three times as many chose "doing what you want, when you want, and not having to answer to anyone" as the best way to live than "never losing sight of what's really important." In essence they are saying, "It's okay to lose sight of what's important as long as you get to do what you want." How would that mind-set work for your team or company or family?

What I find most interesting from the list is the lack of comprehensive strategy. The list is random. But the majority of the individual items are also quite random. The truth is, most people approach their lives quite randomly, and yet we often expect them to approach their work strategically. This is one of the great disconnects of the modern corporate world. It is unreasonable to expect an employee to do something for the business that he is not willing to do for his life. It would be a mistake for me to hire someone to balance my books and do my accounting if that person could not balance her own checkbook.

Learning to live strategically is the first step toward working strategically, and most people in the workforce today lack this fundamental life skill. It doesn't make them bad people. They were never taught. But it is in the best interest of every company to train their employees to live strategically. In fact, it can be argued that all other training is a waste of time, effort, and resources, until we are taught to live strategically.

A More Strategic Approach

The reason we don't train employees to live strategically is that we consider this skill to be a personal matter. Maybe it is, but that personal matter is having an enormous impact on our professional capacity . . . and on our organizations. So again we discover that the ties between the personal and professional are undeniable. For similar reasons, in corporate culture we avoid the question "How is the best way to live?" On one hand, we say it is a personal matter. This is true, but it is a personal matter that has tremendous impact on the organization. On the other hand, we say that the answer to this question is different for everyone. That is only partially true.

Certainly we cannot consider the question "How is the best way to live?" in a vacuum, but in a real place and time, for a specific person, with roles and responsibilities, needs, hopes, and desires. With this in mind we tend to leap straight to the conclusion that the best way to live is different for everyone. But is it? The answer, I think, is yes and no. A more strategic approach to this ageless question has to consider what is common to everyone before we leap to what is unique to each individual.

On some level the best way to live is the same for all of us. I would like to propose three principles common to all men and women of goodwill.

The First Principle

The first principle is simply this: you are here to become the-best-version-of-yourself. It would seem clear that you are not here to become a second-rate-version-of-yourself. Nor are you here to be another version of your parents, teachers, friends, or siblings. At some very basic foundational level you are here to be yourself. Being yourself is much more difficult than most would suppose, however, because it requires the real work of self-discovery. Nonetheless, in this you share a common bond with all men, women, and children, for we are all here to become the-best-version-of-ourselves. The best way to live, therefore, is in such ways that help you become the-best-version-of-yourself.

This first principle serves not only as a basis upon which to begin to answer the question about the best way to live, but also as a very practical guide to the choices that make up everyday life. In fact, I would go as far as to say that everything in life (and business) makes sense in relation to this single principle. A good friend is someone who helps you become the-best-version-of-yourself. The best meals are those that involve food and company that help you become the-best-version-of-yourself. Good books, movies, and music are those that inspire you to become the-best-version-of-yourself. The purpose of education is to help you become the-best-version-of-yourself. The primary meaning of work is not to make money; rather, when you work hard and pay attention to the details of your work, you develop character and become a-better-version-of-yourself. Marriage is two people encouraging and challenging each other to become the-best-version-of-themselves and raising children and encouraging them to become the-best-version-of-themselves.

Everything makes sense in relation to the first principle. Life is about saying yes to the things that help you become the-best-version-of-yourself and no to the things that don't. It is not more complicated than that. Of course, we manage to complicate it quite a deal more. On a different plane of thinking the concept becomes a thing of beauty, for we finally realize that anyone or anything that does not help us to become a-better-version-of-ourselves is just too small for us. What liberation and joy we experience when we make this truth our own for the very first time.

The first principle also has its place in the business world. Imagine a team that is consumed with the question "How can this team become the-best-version-of-itself?" Imagine an employee who is constantly asking herself, "What can I do today to help this company become the-best-version-of-itself?" The best employees and managers, the best teams, and the best companies are consumed with this type of thinking.

This concept of celebrating the-best-version-of-ourselves at different moments and in different situations throughout the day brings the philosophical question about the best way to live to a very real and practical level. As our awareness grows we become mindful that we are constantly making choices and that every choice causes us to become a-better-version-of-ourselves or a-lesser-version-of-ourselves.

If we accept the first principle, then the meaning-of-life conversation becomes a fairly short one. You are here to become the-best-version-of-yourself. We all have this in common, so the best way to live, on a macro level for everyone, is by making an effort to become the-best-version-of-ourselves. Thus, on one level the answer to the question "How is the best way to live?" is the same for us all.

The Second Principle

For thousands of years great thinkers, including Plato, Aristotle, Augustine, Aquinas, Duns Scotus, Descartes, Kant, Marcus Aurelius, Epictetus, have held, each in his own way, that "virtue" is the best way to live. This idea holds true today for all of us; virtue is the second principle.

Every culture, country, and organization has an organizing principle. For Hitler's Germany it was tyranny. For Castro's Cuba it is dictatorship. For the United States it is law, which supports democracy and capitalism. For many companies it is reward. For some organizations it is excellence or contribution. For others it is fear.

But what is the ultimate organizing principle—for your life, your family, an organization, a country, or, indeed, all of humanity? Virtue. Not necessarily in a religious sense but simply in the broader, classical Greek sense of the word.

Consider this. Two patient people will always have a better relationship than two impatient people. Two generous people will always have a better relationship than two selfish people. Two courageous people will always have a better relationship than two cowardly people. Two humble people will always have a better relationship than two prideful people. And every aspect of society—in a family, among a community, within an organization, or even between nations—is an extension and multiplication of this single relationship.

Think of it in this way. Who would you prefer as your employees or colleagues: men and women of virtue or those riddled with vice and selfishness? Would you prefer your neighbors be patient or impatient? Would you rather your extended family be generous or self-seeking? Would you prefer honest or dishonest customers? Would you rather have a courageous or a cowardly manager?

The whole world prefers virtue.

In the world of business we may be tempted to say that virtue is a personal matter. Indeed, in some ways it is, but again the virtue of a company's employees has an enormous impact on every aspect of the business. The virtue of a company is not measured by its mission and vision statements, nor is it measured by a company's stated values. The virtue of a company is measured by the collective virtue of its employees, managers, and leadership. It would also be a mistake to think that virtue is not necessary for success in business. You may experience short-term gains without virtue. Indeed, vice may even exaggerate those short-term gains. But the discipline of virtue is at the very heart of any long-term success.

Virtue is the essence of excellence in both life and business. So, in virtue, we have another example of how the best way to live is the same for us all.

The Third Principle

The third principle is simply self-control. The best way to live is with self-control. Self-control may very well be man's highest need. Without it we are rendered incapable of any sustainable success in life, business, or relationships. For without self-control we are incapable of delaying gratification. Individualism, hedonism, and minimalism all lead to the decay of a person's self-control and the demise of his or her ability to delay gratification.

There is no success without the ability to delay gratification. What happens to a woman's personal finances if she lacks the ability to delay gratification? What type of relationships is a man likely to have if he lacks the ability to delay gratification? What quality of work can you expect from a person unwilling or unable to delay gratification? What will happen to the health and well-being of a person who refuses ever to delay gratification?

Now, I am not saying that we should always delay gratification. I am simply saying that in order to live your best life it is a required skill.

In these three principles—you are here to become the-best-version-of-yourself, virtue is the ultimate organizing principle, and self-control is central to the best way to live—we find the common elements that bind us all together in our quest to answer the question "How is the best way to live?" It is better to live in such a way that helps you become the-best-version-of-yourself rather than to live in a way that diminishes you and makes you less than who you are. It is better to live a life of virtue than a life of vice. And it is better to live with self-control than without it.

Most people's knowledge of and dedication to these three principles is minimal. At the same time, their dedication to the philosophies of individualism, hedonism, and minimalism dwarfs their commitment to these three principles. There lies the challenge of modern management and leadership.

To an extent, however, the best way to live differs from person to person and at different times of our lives.

The best way for a single person to live may be legitimately very different from the best way for a married person to live. One of my passions is helping young people discover their mission in life. This is the major work of my charitable foundation. When I have the chance to speak to high school and college students, one of my regular themes surrounds engaging "singleness."

We never have a better opportunity to serve than when we are single. Most people go on to marry, and marriage brings with it a series of commitments and responsibilities that limit our ability to serve people, causes, and organizations beyond our immediate duties. But in our singleness we can serve generously almost without reserve and in ways that simply would not be possible for a married person.

On a personal level, when I was single the best way for me to live was to be actively involved in a variety of community and charitable organizations. Now that I am married and raising my family, I would be irresponsible as a husband and father to be involved in these volunteer activities to the same extent. It would not be the best way to live, because it would be giving priority to something that is secondary. My primary responsibilities now are as a husband and a father.

In the same way, the best way to live can change as we move through the various seasons of life. What is the best way to live at thirty years old may differ at forty, fifty, sixty, and seventy. This is true even though our primary roles and responsibilities may not change through these different seasons.

And so, in delving into the question "How is the best way to live?" we quickly discover that it is not a question that we ask once, answer once, and are finished with. It is a dynamic question that requires a little bit of our attention every day, week, month, year, and decade of our lives.

So it is that, while the first principle provides a framework and the great philosophers provide compelling insight about the universal role of virtue, the question remains a deeply personal one.

This leads us straight to what may be the single largest deficiency in the work-life balance quest of the past twenty years: personal responsibility. Work-life balance, work-life effectiveness, personal and professional satisfaction—or whatever you choose to call it—is not an entitlement or benefit. Your company cannot give it to you. You have to create it for yourself. You are personally responsible for living the best life you can.

You are personally responsible for the speed of your life and your lifestyle. This is a frightening truth because it causes us to realize that we have chosen and created the life we are living right now. But while it may be frightening for us to think that we have chosen to live our life exactly as it is today, it is also liberating. Liberating because, while we may not like what we find when we look at our lives today, we can now begin to choose differently. If we refuse to face this truth, we become victims who are incapable of thriving and must content ourselves with surviving. In this victim mentality we look to other people, our companies, and the government to create for us a better life. And it is from this place of victimhood that too many look to their companies to create work-life balance for them. The mentality of a victim always leads to entitlement rather than empowerment. Men and women who are empowered look to build a bigger future for themselves, their families, their company, and their country. Those who adopt a position of entitlement look to sustain or even advance what they already have with little or no effort. There is no future in entitlement.

How is the best way to live? You alone have to decide for yourself. But decide and pursue that life. Don't just stumble through it. Your employer cannot tell you the best way for you to live, nor can the company you work for create a program that will lead you to an abundant life of personal and professional satisfaction independent of your personal efforts. You and I have to take responsibility for these things ourselves, which is so much better anyway. Wouldn't you rather feel that you have some control over your destiny?

Change the Conversation

In many ways our lives are simply an answer to the questions we are asked and that we ask ourselves. It is true for the life of a person and for the life of a business. In my work as a management consultant, one of my roles is to change the conversation. Sometimes I am required to change the conversation in a board meeting; other times I am required to change the conversation in a strategic planning session; often I am required to change the conversation for a marketing campaign; and occasionally I get to change the conversation for a whole industry. People, businesses, and whole industries often get stuck in the wrong conversations.

The banking industry provides a perfect example. It doesn't seem to matter what city I am in, or what highway I am driving down, I see billboards announcing FREE CHECKING. I have been seeing them for more than a decade. Free checking is no longer a new offer, but the billboards persist.

Now, banking is a highly competitive and massively commoditized industry. That is, the services provided by your bank are widely available and interchangeable with the services provided by every other bank. In such a market, innovation (and hence market dominance) comes not from new products or services but rather from changing the conversation.

The same banking industry spends hundreds of millions of dollars every year on advertising—television advertisements, print media placements, radio spots, and billboards. And what message do they choose to deliver? Free checking. At this point isn't free checking a given? Isn't it clear that if you want free checking, you can get free checking? Someone needs to change the conversation, and the bank that does (and does it properly) will capture market share at an alarming rate.

How would a bank change the conversation? Simple. Easy. A new media campaign. Core message: "What's Your Dream? We Can Help. XYZ Bank." If you are driving to work and you see this message on a billboard, you are going to have a very different reaction than you would to the "Do you want free checking?" message. Both messages contain a question, but one question leads to entitlement and the other leads to empowerment. Are banks in the "free checking" business or the "partnering with customers to fulfill their dreams" business? I know which business I would rather be in.

Sometimes in business we just get stuck on the wrong question. It happens in life too, and when it does you need to change the question.

Your life today is an answer to the questions you have asked up until now. The good news is that you can change the questions anytime you wish. Ask better questions and you get better answers. Sometimes changing our lives can be as simple as changing the questions we habitually ask ourselves and others.

When I was a child everyone asked, "What do you want to do when you grow up?" When I was in high school everyone asked, "What do you want to do in college?" When I was in college everyone asked, "What do you want to do when you graduate?" So I spent a lot of time thinking about what I wanted to do and a lot of time doing what I wanted to do. The question made me think that life was about doing what you wanted to do. I constantly tried to create situations where I could do exactly what I wanted to do, when I wanted to do it. Fortunately, I was quite successful at this and quickly realized that satisfaction was not to be found in doing whatever I wanted to do. I have never found any lasting happiness doing what I wanted to do. But that was the question society kept placing before me, so that was the question I kept asking myself.

As the years have passed other questions have emerged. How is the best way to live? How can I best engage my talents and abilities to make a contribution? What helps me become the-best-version-of-myself? How can I lighten the burden of those less fortunate than myself? Where do I find genuine satisfaction? But in truth, these questions have been slow in surfacing, and it has taken several cycles of chasing what I wanted with reckless abandon, achieving what I wanted, and experiencing a certain emptiness for me to take these other questions more seriously and make them a more constant part of my inner dialogue and reflection. And, even today, I still find myself occasionally falling back into those old questions.

Questions shape our lives. The good news is that if you change the question, you can change your life.

How is the best way to live? It is a beautiful question. Allow this question a place in your inner dialogue. Start to ponder it. Pause deliberately to reflect upon it. Experiment with it. Explore the best way to start your day. Try several ways and note how you feel as your day begins and ends, your energy level rises and falls, your focus and efficiency wax and wane. Once you have discovered the best way to start your day, experiment with the best way to end your day. Having answered this question, you can move on to the best way to live a weekend. How is the best way to live? It is an incredible question, but let me warn you, do not flirt with this question. A casual affair with this question is not enough, and more than that, a casual fling with this question may do more harm than good. The question needs to be approached rigorously and strategically. If you think you are not willing or able to do that, set this book down and do not look back upon it until you are ready to fully embrace the question.

Imagine. What would happen if you started to take this one question seriously? What would happen if you approached this question as strategically as Procter & Gamble approaches the development of a new product or as rigorously as Coca-Cola approaches a new ad campaign? This rigor and strategy are the elements that have been missing from the work-life balance experiment of the past twenty years. This same rigor and strategy are just what this book will help you to adopt so you can design and build a deeply satisfying life—personally and professionally.

How is the best way to live? It is a question that challenges us to consider how we are living our one short life and what is possible. It is a question that challenges our lives to evolve. Perhaps we avoid the question because it just seems overwhelming. When that's the case, we need to remind ourselves that finding the best way to live begins with finding a *better* way to live.

2

How Satisfied Are You?

One of the beautiful things about satisfaction is that you know when you have it and you know when you don't. Satisfaction is also something we can increase with effort. So observing what does and does not lead to satisfaction is critical, and taking stock of our satisfaction level from time to time helps us do that. Take a moment to assess the level of satisfaction in your life. Circle a number between 1 and 10 (10 being completely satisfied; 1 being very dissatisfied).

How satisfied are you personally?

1   2   3   4   5   6   7   8   9   10

How satisfied are you professionally?

1   2   3   4   5   6   7   8   9   10

It may not be very scientific, but it gives you a sense of where you are. This book is about increasing your satisfaction both personally and professionally. Perhaps you know what is required to increase the level of satisfaction in your life, and perhaps you don't. In my experience, many people are mistaken about what they think will lead to greater levels of satisfaction.

My Own Experience

I have to admit, I don't have a very balanced life. I suppose that was part of what led me to be so interested in the whole work-life balance discussion. There are times when I go on the road to speak and consult for a week at a time, and those weeks lack what I think most people would define as work-life balance. Some months are busier than others, and those months lack balance. And some years have more than their fair share of enormous projects and restructuring, and those years certainly lack balance. On the other hand, I have a lot more flexibility than most people, take more vacations than most people, and enjoy my work in a way that very rarely makes me feel overworked.

I don't have balance. The good news is I now know that I don't want balance. What I do want is satisfaction. Both personally and professionally I have a very satisfying life. Am I completely satisfied? No. I don't mind telling you that I am both deeply satisfied and turbulently dissatisfied at times. But even my dissatisfaction drives me toward greater satisfaction in the future.

The truth is, I work more than anybody I know, but I lead a tremendously satisfying life.

One of the lies that the work-life balance conversation unconsciously propagated is the idea that working long, hard hours is bad. The truth is, working really hard at different times of our lives is very good for us. There have been times when I have worked eighty-five-hour weeks for a month at a stretch. There have been times when I have written for three days straight with virtually no sleep. There have been times when I have traveled to one hundred cities in one hundred and twenty days. In school there were times when my mates and I would put in twelve-hour study days every Saturday and Sunday throughout the semester.

I guess what I am trying to say is twofold. First, these were deeply satisfying times in my life in and of themselves. We all need and thrive on the sense of accomplishing something. The sense of accomplishment brings with it the reward of tremendous satisfaction. Second, I want to make clear here that I am not sorry I did these things. I don't regret them. I am not sorry I made these sacrifices. Each experience challenged or encouraged or forced me to develop character. And as important as anything else, each of these choices put me in the room now, and I like being in the room.

What I mean by that is, today I get to work with some of the best companies and the most incredible business minds in the world. I love being in the room, and the truth is, you don't get in *that* room by working forty-hour weeks. If you don't want to be in that room, that's okay. But if you do, regardless of what it is you do or you want to do, chances are, it is going to take more than forty-hour weeks to get you in the room. Let's face it, a forty-hour week is the baseline. So I think it is fair to assume that excellence and market dominance are found somewhere beyond a forty-hour week. I didn't invent the forty-hour week, but it is what it is—the standard. And to ignore that baseline reality is to detach ourselves from the reality, and that never leads to success.

There are some who will say that in this modern age we can work smarter. It's true, but so can everyone else. And some of the people who make up the everyone else are willing to work smarter for fifty, sixty, or seventy hours a week. Don't get me wrong, I am not espousing a sixty-hour workweek. I am just pointing out the reality of our times.

For you, work may just be something you do to pay the bills. You can probably have your forty-hour workweek and keep your professional life relatively compartmentalized. Leave your work at work, so to speak. But your work will probably be less satisfying than you would like. Satisfaction comes from emptying ourselves into things.

The other side of this discussion is that I have also found tremendous satisfaction in stepping back from work. One summer a few years ago I took forty days off to walk the Camino. The Camino is a five-hundred-mile trail that begins in the south of France, comes south across the Pyrenees, and then works its way directly west across the north of Spain, finishing in Santiago. People have been walking this route for more than a thousand years.

I first heard about it in a magazine article. I remember thinking it would be a fabulous adventure, and I am not really the outdoors type. I wrote it in my dream book even though I don't think I ever believed I would do it. Ten years later I flew to southern France with a backpack, a water bottle, a sleeping bag, a map . . . and started walking. I walked on average twenty miles a day. Some days it took ten hours, and some days in the mountains it took sixteen hours. Just walking. No music, no television, and no cell phone. Just walking. Like no other time in my life I completely unplugged from the world.

This was a tremendously satisfying experience. In fact, when I returned from this trip I spent three days with virtually no sleep writing the first draft of *The Dream Manager*. And so times of both intense work and complete detachment from work are part of a deeply satisfying life.

Too often we remove both extremes from our lives and rob ourselves of incredible satisfaction. In particular we are tempted to remove those intense periods of work from our lives—days or weeks when we throw ourselves completely into a project. In doing so we rob ourselves of the intense satisfaction that comes from working on a project in such a way. On the other hand, we also resist completely detaching from the world or work from time to time. The perfect example: we tend to vacation with our cell phones and laptops. When we do this, we rob ourselves of the rejuvenation we need to throw ourselves passionately into our work again when we return.

It's a simple question, and we find it at the very core of the work-life balance discussion. How satisfied are you? Most people would answer the question in vague terms if you asked them. But here's the thing: essentially, satisfaction is what we are all seeking. Where will that satisfaction come from? The answer to this question is usually not what we expect.

Work-Life Balance Champions

These were the ideas that originally sent me looking for the work-life balance champions. I knew that if I could find a variety of people who were really good at work-life balance, then I could study them and help my company's clients help their employees develop superior work-life balance. This would lead to a highly engaged workforce and result in massively competitive teams. This is how this book first came about.

The first thing I did was ask well-respected people within various departments at three dozen of the world's best companies to nominate who they thought was exceptional in the area of work-life balance. I was surprised how easily they pointed them out. My next step was to interview these champions of work-life balance. I interviewed dozens of them, and then dozens more. I delved into their lives, and I was surprised at how open and honest they were about their successes and challenges, both personally and professionally. I could publish a two-hundred-page thesis with my findings, but I will spare you the pain. The bottom-line finding from all these interviews is this: these people are not champions of work-life balance. They certainly are not excelling at what their peers who elected them as work-life balance champions think work-life balance is. On average these supposed champions of work-life balance work nine hours more per week than their counterparts. They work hard and long hours, and they do it intentionally. They also, for the most part, have little or no misgivings about this reality.

So why did their colleagues single them out as champions of work-life balance? The answer is because, as it turns out, with almost all of them, they have large quantities of what this book is really about—personal and professional satisfaction. They work hard, but they have a sense of satisfaction when they leave the office after a long day. This professional satisfaction is fueled by several factors: they enjoy the people they work with; they feel respected by their boss; they feel their work is making a contribution to customers' lives; they find the challenge of their work matches their abilities; and they know why they go to work each day. This last one is critical, and it provides the segue into the personal realm. You see, people don't come to work because they love their company, their work, or their boss. They may love all these things, but these are not the primary reasons they come to work. People come to work because they have dreams for themselves and for their families. And those who are achieving high levels of personal and professional satisfaction know what those dreams are. For some it is a vision for retirement, but not for many. For most it has a lot to do with giving their children a first-rate experience of life and every chance to succeed for themselves. For others it is a vision of a second career in their early to midfifties . . . which often is the thing they always really wanted to do.

I didn't find any work-life balance champions out there who manage to deliver in equal measure to the personal and professional aspects of their life. I didn't find men and women who could completely control every realm of their life so as to allocate perfectly equal portions of time, energy, and attention to both the personal and the professional. No, I didn't find these people. But I did find men and women achieving at high levels professionally who have amazing personal lives also. And I found people who are filled with a profound sense of satisfaction. Pinpointing the satisfaction and having the opportunity to be around it made me want to bottle it and share it with everyone I could. Those interviews had a profound effect on me and completely changed what this book is ultimately about.

What Is Satisfaction?

If you ask people why they want work-life balance, they talk about things that have little or nothing to do with balance. They talk about dynamic relationships, fulfilling careers, challenging projects that engage their talents, opportunities to grow as a whole person, and pursuing their personal and professional dreams. The reason people ostensibly talking about work-life balance end up talking about anything but balance is because the term has become the catchall for people's dissatisfaction. What people start talking about is what will bring satisfaction to their lives.

The people, places, things, and activities that lead to satisfaction may differ from person to person, but a dictionary definition of "satisfaction" is a great place to start. The *American Heritage Dictionary* defines it as:

1. a. The fulfillment or gratification of a desire, need, or appetite.

   b. Pleasure or contentment derived from such gratification.

   c. A source or means of gratification.

What is satisfaction? The contentment and fulfillment that arise from the gratification of needs and desires.

We will speak more of this, but for now it is enough to point out that satisfaction that emerges in response to the fulfillment of a need tends to be a lasting satisfaction, while satisfaction that is the result of the gratification of a desire tends to have a much shorter shelf life. Both are necessary to live a deeply fulfilling life, but the fulfillment of needs is primary and the gratification of desires is secondary.

What the definition does not say is that there is a spectrum of satisfaction. I eat a burger and I feel satisfied. I help my son learn or experience something for the first time, and I have a different level of satisfaction.

Satisfaction is different for everyone. What brings me satisfaction may drive you crazy. What brings you satisfaction may bore me to death. This is why it is the personal responsibility of each person to create satisfaction. Nonetheless, the nature of the things that lead to satisfaction are the same for each person.

Here we encounter the first principle again. Interestingly enough, the things that tend to bring lasting satisfaction in an ever-changing world are the things that help us become the-best-version-of-ourselves.

Note that personal and professional satisfaction differs from work-life balance in two critical ways. First, satisfaction is possible. Will you be completely satisfied all the time? No. But it is possible, and we know it is, because we have all experienced it at some point in our lives and careers. However briefly, we have experienced it, and so we know it. Having known it, we can reproduce it. Second, satisfaction is much easier to sustain. To maintain balance, as the work-life balance conversation has framed it, requires the creation of an artificial environment in which you can control many of the things that you simply cannot control. Satisfaction can be created and maintained in a much more dynamic and unpredictable environment.

Now, what is *not* satisfaction? Two of the main features commonly associated with the work-life balance have little to do with satisfaction. Satisfaction is not necessarily getting what you want, and it is not merely pleasure.

Getting what you want is great, but it's not always possible, so if we define satisfaction in terms of it, I suspect we are in for a great deal of dissatisfaction. If it is to be sustained, our satisfaction has to be something that transcends external circumstance. It cannot be something that we put in the hands of things that are completely beyond our control.

Nor is satisfaction the mere attainment of pleasure. Interestingly, the greatest experience of satisfaction often comes after times of great stress and even intense suffering (of one kind or another). And any experience of satisfaction almost always follows some type of delayed gratification. Instant gratification is not a path to lasting satisfaction. Perhaps that is why Mick Jagger never could get any satisfaction.

Measuring It Is Critical

I hope by now I am starting to convince you that you should make the pursuit of personal and professional satisfaction a priority in your life. With that in mind, I have to counsel you to begin to measure it in some way. The thing that continually amazes me about the very best companies in the world is that they measure everything. And every time I think they cannot possibly measure anything else, they come up with something new to measure that drives their business to a new level.

If you cannot measure something, you cannot change it. Measuring something is critical to the process of change and improvement. So to increase the level of satisfaction in your life you need to find a way to measure it. To help with this, I offer the following assessment exercise as your next step. These twenty questions are designed to measure your satisfaction levels in relation to different aspects of your life within both the personal and the professional realm. I encourage you not to overthink the questions; simply take a quick gut check and answer without rushing but without prolonged reflection.

1. Disposition

a. I feel miserable almost all the time.

b. I often feel miserable.

c. I usually feel neutral.

d. I usually feel pretty good.

e. I feel great almost all the time.

2. Interest

a. I find life boring all the time.

b. I'm pretty bored with most aspects of my life.

c. I find life boring at times, but at other times it interests me.

d. I'm interested in most aspects of life.

e. I find life and living to be absolutely fascinating.

3. Purpose

a. I have no direction or life purpose.

b. I'm unsure about my life direction and purpose.

c. Sometimes I feel as if I know my life purpose.

d. I'm pretty clear about my life purpose and direction.

e. My life purpose and direction are crystal clear.

4. Overall Energy

a. I have no energy and feel tired almost all the time.

b. I often feel tired and lethargic.

c. I usually have enough energy to do what I need to do.

d. Most of the time I feel energetic and enthusiastic.

e. I'm bursting with energy and enthusiasm almost all the time.

5. The Future

a. I'm extremely pessimistic about the future.

b. There are times when I feel pessimistic about the future.

c. I'm not sure about the future one way or another.

d. I'm pretty optimistic about the future.

e. I'm extremely optimistic and excited about the future.

6. Friendship

a. I don't have any close friends.

b. I have a few friends but none I consider really close.

c. I have a few good friends and family members with whom I am close.

d. I have quite a few good friends.

e. I have lots of friends and easily connect with everyone.

7. Talents and Abilities

a. I don't think I have any strengths at all.

b. I'm not sure whether or not I have any strengths.

c. I'm getting to know my strengths.

d. I know my strengths and try to use them when I can.

e. I know exactly what my strengths are and use them all the time.

8. Enjoyment

a. I never enjoy myself no matter what I'm doing.

b. I find it difficult to enjoy life in the moment.

c. I try to enjoy life as much as I can.

d. I enjoy myself most of the time.

e. I thoroughly enjoy every moment.

9. Gratitude

a. I have absolutely nothing for which to be grateful.

b. There's not much in my life for which I'm grateful.

c. I'm grateful for a few things in my life.

d. I have quite a few things in my life for which to be grateful.

e. I'm extremely grateful for many things in my life.

10. Accomplishment

a. I've accomplished nothing.

b. I've not accomplished much in life.

c. I've accomplished about as much as the average person.

d. I've accomplished more in life than most people.

e. I've accomplished a great deal more in life than most people.

11. General Work Enjoyment

a. I am miserable at work all the time.

b. I find it difficult to enjoy my work.

c. I try to enjoy work as much as I can.

d. I enjoy my work most of the time.

e. I am passionate about my work and thoroughly enjoy it.

12. Attitude

a. I hate going to work.

b. I go to work only for the money.

c. I sometimes enjoy going to work.

d. Usually I enjoy going to work.

e. I love going to work.

13. Energy after Work

a. When I come home from work I am exhausted and cannot do anything meaningful.

b. When I come home from work I often feel tired and lethargic.

c. When I come home from work I usually have enough energy to do what I need to do.

d. Most of the time when I come home from work I feel energetic and enthusiastic.

e. I almost always have energy for the things I like to do when I come home from work.

14. Fulfillment at Work

a. I hate the work I do.

b. I don't mind the work I do, but it adds no value.

c. Occasionally I enjoy my work.

d. More often than not I enjoy my work.

e. I almost always enjoy my work. It challenges and stimulates me, and I feel it adds value.

15. Colleagues

a. I cannot stand my colleagues.

b. Occasionally I want to quit my job because of my colleagues.

c. My colleagues are not the best, but they are not the worst.

d. I usually feel pretty good about my colleagues.

e. I love working with my colleagues; they support me personally and professionally.

16. My Manager

a. My manager is not at all interested in me as a person.

b. My manager shows occasional interest in my life and career.

c. My manager has my interests at heart as long as they do not conflict with his or her interests or the company's.

d. My manager has my best interests at heart.

e. My manager goes out of his or her way to help me develop personally and professionally.

17. My Company

a. I am never enthusiastic about the company I work for.

b. I find it difficult to be enthusiastic about the company I work for.

c. I try to be enthusiastic about the company I work for.

d. Most of the time I am enthusiastic about the company I work for.

e. I am extremely enthusiastic about the company I work for.

18. Career

a. I don't have a career, I have a job.

b. I almost never feel good about the direction of my career.

c. Sometimes I feel good about my career direction, and sometimes I don't.

d. Most of the time I feel good about the direction of my career.

e. I am more than confident that my career is moving in the right direction.

19. Other Job Offers

a. I should be looking for another job, but I am procrastinating.

b. I am actively looking for another job.

c. If offered another job I would be very interested.

d. If I got offered another job I would listen to what they had to say but I probably would not be interested.

e. I have no interest at all in another job; if offered I would not even consider it.

20. Engagement

a. I have quit mentally but remain physically. I am almost completely disengaged from my work.

b. Often I am disengaged from my work.

c. Occasionally I am disengaged.

d. Every now and then I feel myself disengaging, but for the most part I am highly engaged in my work.

e. I am totally engaged—passionate about what I do.

Satisfaction Scorecard

A = 1   B = 2   C = 3   D = 4   E = 5

Question No.	Score	Question No.	Score
1		11	
2		12	
3		13	
4		14	
5		15	
6		16	
7		17	
8		18	
9		19	
10		20	
Subtotal A		Subtotal B	

Subtotal A = Personal Satisfaction Score

Subtotal B = Professional Satisfaction Score

A + B = Personal and Professional Satisfaction (PPS) Score

The highest possible combined score is 100. The lowest possible combined score is 20.

If your Personal Satisfaction score is:

10–20: You are experiencing deep levels of dissatisfaction in the personal aspects of your life.

21–39: You are experiencing moderate levels of personal satisfaction. It would be very beneficial to review the questions in which you scored poorly and focus on increasing satisfaction in those areas of your personal life.

40–50: You are leading a deeply satisfying personal life, and while there may be ways you can increase the satisfaction you are experiencing, more important is to recognize how to sustain the satisfaction you are currently enjoying.

If your Professional Satisfaction score is:

10–20: You are experiencing deep levels of dissatisfaction in the professional aspects of your life.

21–39: You are experiencing moderate levels of professional satisfaction. It would be very beneficial to review the questions in which you scored poorly and focus on increasing satisfaction in those areas of your professional life.

40–50: You are leading a deeply satisfying professional life, and while there may be ways you can increase the satisfaction you are experiencing, more important is to recognize how to sustain the satisfaction you are currently enjoying.

The Personal and Professional Satisfaction Assessment is available online at FloydConsulting.com. I encourage you to take the assessment once every three months for the next year, and twice a year after that, to track your progress. The online assessment will also provide you with a series of personalized suggestions to help you improve your satisfaction score in various areas of your life.

The Connection between the Personal and Professional

Some people have decided that professional satisfaction is not possible. They tell themselves that they will just grin and bear it at work and instead focus on personal satisfaction. This never works, for the same reason corporate efforts to have employees leave their personal lives at home never work.

It is impossible to completely separate the personal from the professional.

For hundreds of years, almost from the beginning of corporate history, a divide between the personal life and professional life has been asserted. This is a false divide. There are certainly boundaries between the two, but even they are blurry and easily crossed, consciously or unconsciously.

If you get done at work today and decide to eat two extra-large pizzas with extra cheese, a couple of two-liter bottles of Coke, a large tub of ice cream, and some chicken wings for dinner, you will become a-lesser version-of-yourself and your company will become a-lesser-version-of-itself. On the other hand, if you get done with work and decide to exercise and afterward have a dinner filled with fresh foods that nourish you perfectly, you will become a-better-version-of-yourself and your company will become a-better-version-of-itself. It is impossible to separate the personal from the professional; the two are intricately linked.

If you have a sick child at home today, you will be distracted and to some extent disengaged from your work. If that were not the case, I would be worried. If great things are happening for you and your team at work, you take that fabulous energy home with you to your family. If you are under enormous pressure at work and things are not going as you, your team, your boss, or your customers would like, you bring that stress home with you, and everyone can sense that . . . even your dog.

In the industrial age we told workers to leave their personal lives at home. In return we did not require them to think about their work outside a nine-to-five schedule. But this was always a charade. If a factory worker comes to work with personal problems, a sick wife or child, financial pressures, or marital problems, isn't that worker many times more likely to have an accident on the job? Separating the personal from the professional sounds good in theory, but in practice it just doesn't work. It's a little like the new formula for Coke or Crystal Pepsi—in theory they seemed like great ideas. The best companies in the world spent hundreds of millions of dollars developing, testing, branding, and marketing these products—and they completely failed. Competent people were involved and in charge, but still they flopped. You can add to the list work-life balance and the idea of separating the personal from the professional. In theory they sound great. In reality, they just don't work.

The personal and professional lives of your employees are intimately linked. This is perhaps the scariest reality a manager or business leader can face. Sure, it starts off very innocently, but it can quickly escalate to a place that most people are not comfortable going. It can very quickly end up in a place bordering on being politically incorrect, never mind that it may be true. Let me give you some examples. An employee that works out on a regular basis is likely to be more engaged and more effective in his or her work—not to mention less of a drag on the company's health insurance. The company cannot force an employee to work out, but if the employee does, then the company benefits. Now consider this. An employee is having marital trouble. There is a real cost to the company for that marital strife. An employee's wife dies, leaving him to raise their three children alone. You better believe this is going to affect his ability to contribute at work. An employee's father gets sick and he or she becomes part-time caregiver. The impact on work is inevitable. A child or spouse develops an addiction. This brings major stress, and you can be sure it will negatively affect a person's work. An employee's pet gets sick and needs several visits to the vet over the course of three or four weeks. This will affect work and the company.

Employees with highly functional personal lives are a tremendous asset to a company.

All of these are common occurrences in the life of a company. Many of them are daily or weekly occurrences in a company of any size. Now for the politically incorrect part. Some people bring some of these issues upon themselves—and that may be a matter of character. In which case hiring an employee of impeccable character has a significant impact on the bottom line, and hiring an employee of questionable character is likely to cost your company in more ways than one. But it is considered politically incorrect, and in some cases it is illegal, to delve into certain aspects of a potential employee's character and personal life.

Sure, you can control the amount of time an employee spends at work, but you cannot control the level of focus, efficiency, or engagement. And what is happening in an employee's personal life can cause massive swings in the areas of engagement, focus, and efficiency. Again, the personal is affecting the professional.

It is impossible to separate the destiny of a company from the collective destinies of its people. Their destinies are linked.

If you had to choose between balance and satisfaction, which would you choose? I suspect you would choose satisfaction. Before we all started talking about work-life balance, did anyone wake up in the middle of the night yearning for balance? I don't know. What I am sure of is that if you give me the choice between balance and satisfaction, I choose satisfaction every time. Now, in an attempt to get beyond the limitations of the work-life balance concept, many companies have abolished the term and replaced it with "work-life effectiveness." But again, if you ask me to choose between effectiveness and satisfaction, I choose satisfaction every time. Whether or not people ever really wanted balance is something we could argue about forever, but give people the choice between balance and satisfaction, and I think you will find everyone chooses satisfaction. After all, there is no point to having balance if you are not satisfied. And if you have satisfaction and don't have balance, I guess it turns out you didn't need it after all. It is time to change the work-life balance conversation into a conversation about satisfaction.

How satisfied are you? When I first started asking people this question, these are some of the common answers I got.

"Fairly satisfied . . . I think."

"More satisfied than most."

"Not sure."

"I never think about it."

"Is anybody?"

"Nobody is satisfied. Those who say that they are, are lying."

"Yes."

I would then ask the people who said they were satisfied how they knew. They usually just smiled and said something like, "You just know."

Are you satisfied? If you aren't, what's getting between you and a deeply satisfying life both personally and professionally? Is this the most satisfying time in your life? Can it be? If not, why not?

3

Can You Have It All?

It is a common and childish mistake to believe that satisfaction is all about getting what we want. In truth, we have all gotten what we want on many occasions and not been satisfied. The very basis of satisfaction is a value structure, or a set of priorities, around which to live your life. Can you have it all? Any reasonable person knows the answer to this question is no. It is one of the earliest lessons we learn in childhood, and yet most of us as adults can be quite childish at times. The reason you cannot have it all is not because you are ill-equipped for life or you lack talent or you don't have enough money. It is simply because one of the governing principles of the universe dictates that there are an infinite number of possibilities for any day, year, or life—and every day, year, or life is finite. So part of growing to maturity, part of growing up, requires that we recognize and accept that we cannot have it all.

Most of us recognize that we cannot have it all, but often we subconsciously fall back into moments of nonacceptance. We know we can't have it all, but we refuse to accept that. You can see how this kind of pattern could lead to a great deal of frustration at the very least and real insanity if taken to the extreme.

The work-life balance discussion has failed to adequately make clear that you cannot have it all. Just because we started talking about work-life balance and encouraging it does not mean that people can all of a sudden have everything. I cannot play tennis and golf at the same time. The finite nature of a certain period of time requires that I choose to play tennis or golf this afternoon. I cannot do both at once. We have to choose between many options in deciding what to do on any given day or in any given hour.

The other way this idea plays out is that excellence in any field requires that we miss out on other things. If you want to be the best tennis player in the world, you are going to have to sacrifice a great many other things in order to achieve that. Hopefully, you will decide with a clear head that the things you are giving up are less important than becoming the best tennis player in the world. Success always has required and always will require sacrifice. If success were easy, it would be common. It is difficult and that is why it is rare. More people have the talent than you would think. Few are willing to make the necessary sacrifices. This is an easy example because it is far from us. But let us bring it closer to make it real and personal. To be the best marketing executive in the world requires sacrifice; to be the best HR contact, the best salesperson, the best manager, the best employee, the best account manager . . . all require sacrifice, and I am not sure that the work-life balance discussion of the last twenty years has adequately pointed out that excellence in any field requires sacrifice.

Perhaps you have no desire to be the best at what you do. Perhaps work is just work, something you have to do. In that state of mind you will find it very difficult to experience professional satisfaction, and that will be sure to have an impact on your personal satisfaction, as the two are intimately linked. Nonetheless, let's bring the example one step closer, perhaps uncomfortably close.

A mother (or father) who works outside the home cannot expect to be able to do everything for her children that a mother who stays at home does. That does not necessarily mean she is a bad mother or that her children are worse off. But the simple fact remains that her work will require a certain amount of time, energy, and attention—all of which cannot be given to both work and her children. She may have plenty of time, energy, and attention for her children outside of work. Only she can decide that. But the mother who does not work will by simple math have more time, energy, and attention to give her children. The reality is that a working mother cannot expect to do everything a stay-at-home mother does. There are trade-offs that need to be made.

In a way the work-life balance discussion has made us feel that we can have it all, and we cannot. Most people don't want to hear this, and certainly our culture tells us incessantly that we can have it all, but the truth is, you can't. You cannot be in two places at one time, you cannot have it all, and so you must choose.

Learning to Choose . . . Again!

For twenty years now I have been writing, but last year I wrote my first book for children. You pick up a children's book that has a sentence or two on a page and you think, "How hard could that be?" I discovered: harder than you think. Added to that, the subject I had chosen was the meaning of life, and now I had the monumental challenge of explaining to children between the ages of six and ten the meaning of life in four hundred words or less. The title of the book is *Why Am I Here?* It is a story about Max, a seven-year-old, and his quest to discover the meaning of life. With the help of his grandfather and their fishing adventures together, Max discovers that the meaning of life is for each of us to become the-best-version-of-ourselves! In the following days and weeks Max faces a series of situations where he has to choose between the people, places, things, and activities that help him become the-best-version-of-himself and those that do not.

I chose this topic and story line for my first children's book because of two beliefs I hold: passion for life emerges from clarity surrounding our purpose, and learning to make great choices is integral to leading a rich and fulfilling life. Interestingly, we spend alarmingly little time learning about these things in school.

When we don't have a clear sense of purpose we tend to become paralyzed by indecision. I suspect we have all worked for a manager, or witnessed one, who refused to make decisions. He seemed paralyzed by indecision. Either he lacked the courage to choose and act, he lacked clarity about the purpose of the team or project, or he simply did not know what he wanted. Either way, everyone suffers around a person like that. Frustration levels continually rise and eventually people begin to disengage.

In college I had a friend who could not say no to anything because he was scared of missing out on something. His life was utter chaos. He was constantly overcommitted, always disappointing people because he could not possibly fulfill all the commitments he had agreed to, and was usually operating on too little sleep. He didn't realize that he could not do it all.

Do we know how to make choices? Are we aware of our choices when we are making them? Are we conscious that when we say yes to one thing we automatically say no to everything else? Did we ever really learn to make choices?

We make choices every day, hundreds of them. The ability to make good choices is critical to the success of our lives and our businesses. And yet, evidence suggests that few people have ever really been trained to make choices. And when we look at some of the choices people are making in their personal lives, shouldn't we cringe at the fact that they are probably using the same decision-making process to make choices that affect the future and destiny of our business? It seems to me that most of us need to learn how to make choices again.

In Search of Priorities

My life and career have been filled with incredible opportunities that often make me stop and look again. I am often overwhelmed by the people and experiences that make up any given week, and yet the most extraordinary experiences still tend to come when I least expect them. It was that way on a cold morning in Boston last winter. I have never confined myself exclusively to the Fortune 500 space; my partners and I also very much enjoy working with small and medium-size companies. Nonetheless, I spend a lot of time working with Fortune 500 companies. They are all different and they are all the same, and it is a fascinating world. But having done as much work as

I have with various corporations, I must say, I am very rarely surprised.

I had been invited by one of America's premier companies to speak to a group of its midlevel managers who had been chosen as rising stars within the organization. The seminar was to be based on my book *The Dream Manager* and specifically focused on the issue of employee engagement. But for thirty-five minutes, in the middle of my four-hour session, a senior executive was going to speak to the group about work-life balance and how it relates to employee engagement.

Taking my seat in the back of the room I didn't know what to expect, but I will admit I was a bit nervous about what direction his time with the group might take. For the sake of anonymity let's say his name was Tom. I had met him for a few minutes earlier that day. He seemed quiet and introverted, and, to be honest, I wondered if he could hold the group's attention. To say that he held the group's attention would be a massive understatement. He captivated the audience. Within forty-five seconds of when he first opened his mouth I was reaching for my notepad. I took more notes in that thirty-five minutes than during any speech I attended last year. It was powerful.

"I don't know if I have work-life balance. I do know I like my life. I enjoy my work, I have a rewarding family life, and both are important to me." The audience was shifting in their seats, still settling down a little, still sizing him up.

"What I can tell you is that it wasn't always that way. A few years ago all I did was work. I was on the road incessantly, had gotten out of shape, and wasn't even aware that my marriage was in trouble." He had them now. The room was silent. He had made himself personally vulnerable in a way that the corporate world doesn't see enough of, and people were listening. "My wife sat me down one day and told me she didn't think our marriage was working, and that she felt like we were chasing different things. That was perhaps the scariest moment in my life.

"My life is very different today. The reason is that I have worked hard to figure out what really matters to me and have developed a value structure. My priority list is fairly simple: faith, marriage, children, health, and work. It took me a while to make the list, but since I made it I have carried a copy with me everywhere, and the list has become a guide and touchstone in times of decision.

"Now, the first thing I want to make clear is that this is my value structure and priority list. Yours may very well be different, but you should all have one. And it is up to you to figure out what your priorities are.

"It goes without saying, of course, that there have been times since I put this list together ten years ago that I have unnecessarily violated my priorities. Sometimes I did it unconsciously and at other times I did it consciously, deceiving myself into believing that it was absolutely necessary and unavoidable. All this has served to teach me what I consider to be the first law of your value structure: don't mortgage your higher priorities for your lower priorities. Keep the list in front of you. Keep it especially close when making decisions.

"What I discovered when I started to work on my priorities was that my priorities had not changed for many years. I was just ignoring them. So, from time to time now, I reflect upon my priorities and I ask myself, "Could anyone gather enough evidence to prove that these were my priorities? Could a jury of my peers convict me of having these priorities?"

"At the same time, it is important to recognize that the lower priorities can be positive enablers of the higher priorities. For example, health is an enabler of everything else. When I am taking time to work out and eat the right kinds of foods, I am a better husband, father, employee, and manager. In a similar way, work enables me to do certain things in my marriage and with my family that are incredibly positive. The money I earn provides opportunities for my wife and children. My wife is proud of the work I do, and that contributes to the health of our marriage. My work also enriches my faith life by allowing me to contribute generously with our financial resources, but work also enables me to contribute certain skills to my church community. Work fuels the sharing of my time, talent, and treasure with all who cross my path. Another example of how the lower priorities feed and strengthen the higher priorities is found in the fulfillment I find at work. When my work life is fulfilling, I am a better husband and father. Additionally, the incredible training and development opportunities that my company provides make me a better husband, father, member of my community, and citizen.

"With my priorities firmly identified, my actions are not just things I choose to do—they are value statements. I do certain things because I value certain things. At the same time, it is important to recognize that value statements are not time allocation statements. Faith, marriage, and my children are my highest priorities, but I spend more time at work each day than I spend directly with any of these top three priorities. And that's okay. If you try to make your value structure a time allocation structure, I think you will get into trouble pretty quickly. My value structure certainly influences the way I spend my time and what I do, but much more important than that it informs why I do what I do each day.

"Theoretically this all sounds neat, of course, while practically there are real challenges. In the beginning I had to completely reverse engineer the way I had been acting previously. So there were many slipups and some plain old mess-ups. But over time it becomes pretty clear in practical terms. Over time, we start to make logical decisions that we should have been capable of all the time, but in truth they were impossible without the value structure. An example of that is something as simple as having the discipline to leave work at the time that allows me to be home to have dinner with my wife and children. Any sensible person with a view of the whole picture comes to the conclusion that it is better for me to leave work on my desk for tomorrow (or do it later that night) so that I can get home in time for dinner. The reasons are many but here is a basic summary. It is better to leave a little work undone than to have to fix my marriage. And when I say "better," I don't just mean better for me, or for my marriage—but also better for work. Because if my marriage is not in a good place, it is going to drain my energy, distract me from my work, and limit my ability to add value to my team, projects, and company.

"Now, from the very beginning some of you were perhaps perplexed that work was number five on my list. That doesn't mean I don't care about work, or that I don't think my work is important. It is therefore critical to point out that there are dozens of things that didn't even make my list. Take for example friends. My friends didn't make the list, but I consider friendship to be a very important part of life. And yet, in my value structure I place work above friendship. Some people would not agree with that. Before I was married friendships would have ranked above work, but marriage and family shift the priorities we have for the limited social time and energy that is available to us. This is why each of us needs to develop our own value structure and priorities.

"Once we establish our own value structure, or list of priorities, the challenge is to start making choices that honor those values and priorities. It is then that the consequences of our choices become clear. And the consequences of ignoring or betraying our value structure are significant. If I ignore number one, faith, I believe the consequences are eternal. If I mess up number two, marriage, the consequence could be divorce. If I neglect number three, children, I could screw up my kids. If I ignore number four, health, the consequences are fatigue, disease, and premature death. So let's face it, the consequences of messing up number five, work, are minor by comparison. At the end of the day the worst that could happen is I could lose my job and have to find another one.

"At the same time, while work is number five, I want to affirm that I take my work very seriously. I work harder and longer than most, and I am hungry for excellence and results in the professional realm of my life.

"Life is a continuum of choices. We are constantly making choices, and our choices need perspective. Some people talk about deathbed perspective, the idea that you should consider how you might think about a choice when you are on your deathbed, but I don't think you need to go that far. Am I going to sit in a meeting that has run way over its schedule and that I won't even remember ten years from now . . . or leave and get to my son's birthday party? I used to be paralyzed by that choice, but not anymore.

"My value structure helps me to make better choices, and the business benefits from that as well. Because the truth is, if I am making bad choices in my life based on emotion, pressure from others, or other meaningless factors, I am probably making bad choices for the business also. Personal clarity leads to professional clarity. By getting clear about what is really important to me, I have become much better at making choices, which makes me a much greater asset to this company.

"The constant temptation is to think if we flipped the list and made number five, work, our new number one, we would get more done. It's a lie. It's a deception. We might for a day, or a week, or even a month or a quarter, but for any meaningful period of time it is not sustainable. Work all night and see how long it takes before the extra work you got done is lost to downtime, fatigue, or lack of focus. The most efficient people I know, those who consistently get the most done, know how to feed the different areas of their lives, and they don't mortgage their higher priorities for their lower priorities.

"I want to close by sharing three scenarios with you that I think have been important in my journey.

"A couple of years after I committed to this value structure, it was tested in a way that I had not foreseen. I was up for a promotion, and it was for a job that I had always wanted. The process advanced and I knew I was going to be offered the job. When the job offer meeting came around I said to my new-boss-to-be, 'I want this job and I know I can do it very well, but there is something I need you to know before I take the job.' I pulled out my priority list, which I keep in my pocket, and placed it on the table in front of him. He looked at it for a moment and then I continued, 'I will take this new role but I need you to know that these are my priorities, and I will not betray them. At the same time, I want you to know that I will get the job done.' My boss looked at me and said, 'Are you serious about this?' My heart pounded in my chest. 'I am,' I replied. 'Good, because that is exactly the kind of leader I am looking for in this role.'

"The second scenario is more general, and my boss's attitude in the last scenario is a perfect segue. Twenty-five years ago the attitude was you are here to work, so work. At that time there would have been no opportunity for me to share this list with a group like you. And to share it with my boss would have been career suicide. In fact, at that time if this list had fallen into enemy hands, I would never have received another promotion and quite possibly been managed out of the organization or simply fired. In some companies that may still be true; fortunately, it is not here. I'm glad I don't work for a company like that. The corporate world continues to evolve, and while some people think that corporate evolution is always negative in the impact it has on people, I think this is an example of how it is evolving for the better.

"The third scenario requires vulnerability and humility. Once a year I sit down with my wife and she gives me a development plan, in the same way my manager at work does. She gives me a score between one and five in a variety of different areas. We discuss where I am excelling and what opportunities for growth I have. Accountability is the key to the process. We do it at work, and we could not succeed if we didn't have this kind of review and accountability process. So if these other things are more important than work, why don't we have similar processes to help us grow and succeed in the personal aspects of our lives? I invite my wife to hold me accountable, and that is powerful though often humbling."

With that, Tom finished his presentation and answered questions from a highly engaged audience for about twenty minutes.

Do you have a value structure? What are your priorities? In chapter 5 we are going to help each other develop a list just like the one Tom spoke about.

A highly functioning personal life is a tremendous asset to an employee's company. Some people may call this enlightened thinking. I do not. To me it is just common sense. Helping employees develop highly functioning personal lives is simply the best way to lead and manage people.

Continuous Change

Continuous change is now an accepted part of life and business. The waves of change are constantly crashing on the shore of our lives, but it is a well-defined value structure that allows us to thrive in the midst of the change. It is the unchanging that allows us to make sense of the change.

For more than two hundred years America has thrived as a nation in the midst of very different situations and circumstances. How does the United States survive amid the constant change that surrounds her and is within her? The Constitution. When America has a crisis we can look to the Constitution for guidance. When America has an opportunity we can look to the Constitution for direction. In over two hundred years there have been just twenty-seven amendments to this incredible document. If you wrote a mission statement today, you might make twenty-six amendments in the next couple of months. The enduring power of this document comes from the parts of it that are unchanging, and the idea of it that is unchanging.

As individuals we need this unchanging direction also. We discussed earlier that the common unchanging purpose of our lives is to become the-best-version-of-ourselves. In moments of decision, in a crisis, or when presented with an incredible opportunity, you are able to look to this unchanging purpose and ask, "How will this help me to become, or hinder me from becoming, the-best-version-of-myself?"

A defined set of values (or priority list) is a way to deepen and strengthen what is unchanging in our lives. Tom uses his priority list in times of decision because they shine the unchanging light of his priorities on situations that are constantly changing. In the same way, if you take the time to develop your priority list as directed in chapter 5, this list will become a valuable and practical tool in your decision-making process. Let's face it, life is all about choices. We are constantly making choices, but what are we basing our choices on?

We all need some unchanging values and principles to guide us. We live in a world of rapid and continuous change. Such change can be disorienting. The only way to thrive in an environment of change is to know which values are nonnegotiable for you.

Kidnapped by the Urgent

So the bad news is that you cannot have it all. The good news is that you don't really want it all. The even better news is that you can experience incredible levels of satisfaction both personally and professionally if you take the time to work out what matters most to you. In chapter 5 I have laid out a simple process to help you develop your own priority list or value structure.

Without clarity around what matters most, without a clear value and priority structure that we can commit to, our lives tend to get kidnapped by the urgent. By this I simply mean that we give attention and intention to whatever is most urgent. We wake up in the morning and start doing urgent things, and we go to bed at night still doing urgent things. The problem with this is that the most important things are hardly ever urgent. We may have the sense that we are accomplishing many things, but in fact we may be accomplishing very little. The sense of accomplishment is a phantom.

A business can just as easily be kidnapped by the urgent. This is how a company like Sony, which had all the advantages of industry knowledge and owned all the technology and intellectual property it needed to dominate the electronic music market, got overwhelmed by Apple. The examples throughout history are glaring and many. Kodak missed the entry into electronic photography. Why? We get so focused on what is—so focused on what is urgent—that we miss what could be . . . and what matters most.

Without a value structure our lives can get kidnapped by the urgent, and the most important things end up being mortgaged for the least important things. It happens to people, it happens to companies, and it happens to nations. Don't let it happen to you.

4

Batteries Included

How much does a glass of water weigh? When I am conducting training sessions around the whole work-life balance issue I often ask participants this question. "Well, it depends how large or small the glass is," someone always says. "And what the glass is made of," someone else chimes in. So I pick up a glass of water from beneath the podium and ask, "How much does this glass of water weigh?"

"Twelve ounces." "Twenty-four ounces." "No, not that much, eighteen ounces." I let the guessing go on, back and forth, for a minute or so. Then as the crowd quiets down someone usually asks, "How much does it weigh?"

"It depends how long you have to hold it for."

They look at me confused.

So I bring two participants out of the crowd to the front of the room, give them each an identical glass filled with water, and ask them to hold the glass of water straight out in front of them. They usually last about three to five minutes before lowering the glass of water. Occasionally someone will last longer, even significantly longer. But sooner or later the weight of the glass of water becomes intolerable. It's just a glass of water.

Some people can hold the glass for longer than others because some people have more energy than others. In the same way, our experience of life expands with the more energy we have. Think about it. Your capacity for life increases with the more energy you have. Your ability to embrace, absorb, and enjoy all the good things in this world, and your ability to respond and react to the not so good things in this world, depends upon the amount of energy you have.

Of course, many people feel tired most of the time. Most people feel tired by the time they walk through the door at home each night. And a great many people feel tired most days by the middle of the afternoon. This tiredness is not just tiredness; it is a reduced capacity for life.

Next, I ask for a couple more volunteers to come and hold a glass of water. This time I instruct them that they are required to hold the glass of water straight out for one minute at a time, and between those times they are allowed to take a break for twenty seconds. In most cases, they are able to hold the glass for one-minute intervals with twenty-second breaks indefinitely.

Knowing how to balance various activities in our life to

produce the maximum flow of energy is perhaps the most important skill any of us can learn and develop. Each of us has to work out how long we hold the proverbial glass of water in our lives, and each of us needs to determine what sort of breaks we need from holding that glass.

Beyond Time Management

In the latter part of the twentieth century the corporate world seemed obsessed with time management. We took time management courses, listened to audiocassettes (yes, audiocassettes) to hone our time management skills, and read books about the subject too. Over and over we would hear maxims like: Time is your most valuable resource. Guard your time. Plan your time. Protect your time. Defend your time. Don't waste time. Time is life, and life is time. If you waste your time, you are wasting your life. As a result, our time management skills increased exponentially and our ability to deliver results soared.

As with all things, there were early adopters, the mass middle of adoption, and late adopters. The earlier people adopted, honed, and deployed these time management skills, the more of a competitive advantage they were. But time management is no longer a competitive advantage. It is an important and necessary skill but not a competitive advantage. Twenty years ago, the ability to effectively manage your time was a competitive advantage. Today, it is simply permission to play. If you want to compete at a high level in today's environment, it is just expected that you can manage your time more effectively than most people. In the latter part of the twentieth century the discipline of time management increased the effectiveness and productivity of men and women across almost every corporate role by producing an enormous leap in human excellence. But that was then. The real questions are: Where will the next leap in human excellence come from? What will it be? What will drive even higher levels of human performance in the twenty-first century? The answer is: energy management.

Your experience of life expands with the more energy you have. Think about that. I don't write these words lightly. Your experience of life is not a small thing. It is not insignificant. We are not talking about what route you take to work or what you will have for lunch. We are talking about the all-encompassing experience of life. So I will say it again. Your experience of life expands with the more energy you have.

We all know people who seem to squeeze whole lifetimes into a summer. How do they do it? Do they strike you as low-energy people? Is it because they are so good at managing time? I suspect they have more energy than most people. It is not the lazy and the tired who squeeze whole lifetimes into a summer but, rather, men and women who are overflowing with energy and enthusiasm for life.

When did you last feel that way? Seriously, think about it.

When were you last overflowing with energy and enthusiasm for life? Has it been a while? Are you tired of being tired? If so, great! But are you fed up enough to do something about it? Experience tells me you won't change until the pain of not changing is greater than the pain of changing. The only exception to that rule is a life-changing experience. It could be an event. A friend of mine lost his father to cancer, his brother in a car accident, and his best friend to depression and suicide all in two years. The following year he made some radical changes to the way he was living. The life-changing experience could be a seminar, a book, or a new friend. The important thing to realize is that we can change our lives—and change them significantly.

One of my favorite actors is Anthony Hopkins. In *The Edge* he plays a billionaire whose wife and her boyfriend try to murder him. The plot was to take him into the wilderness and kill him there, but the plane is struck by a flock of geese and crashes, leaving Hopkins and his wife's boyfriend stranded in the middle of nowhere. For days they try to make their way back toward civilization, all the while being hunted by a man-eating bear. At one point the wife's boyfriend begins to ramble on about how he is going to change his life. Hopkins stops walking, turns to him, and asks, "Do you know anyone who has really changed their life?" The boyfriend shrugs and Hopkins announces with resolve, "I tell you one thing. I am going to change the way I live."

One very fortunate aspect of the work I do is that I get to see people change, really change. Change in ways that I would not have thought believable. I've seen them change themselves and change their destinies so radically that I can only step back and be inspired.

Most people don't have the energy they need to do the things they love, but they don't have the desire to do anything about it. The great majority of people do not have energy to do the things they love when they come home from work. Some will say it is because they work too hard. Others will say it is because they have so much work to do. But in truth, it is neither of these things. How many millions of people come home from work each night and plant themselves in front of the television for the evening? Not because this is how they want to spend their lives. There are many passions and interests they would rather pursue than plant themselves for hours on end in front of the television each night. But they don't. Why? They don't have the energy.

Worse than that is our inability to recognize the flow of energy in our own lives. So many people look at watching television as a way to rest and relax. But I have to challenge that assumption. Consider your own experience of watching television. When was the last time you got up from watching television with more energy than when you sat down? When was the last time you got done watching television and thought to yourself, "I feel like working out now!" If the next leap in human excellence will be the result of energy management, we need to become infinitely familiar with the people, places, things, and activities that energize us—and equally familiar with the people, places, things, and activities that drain our energy.

Who are the people that energize you? Who drains your energy? What places energize you? Which places drain your energy? What things energize you? Which things drain your energy? What activities energize you? Which activities drain you of your energy?

Being familiar with the people, places, things, and activities that energize you, and those that drain you, is critical to managing your energy. Otherwise you might schedule five people who drain your energy for back-to-back meetings on a Monday morning. The result will be that by the middle of the day on Monday you are drained of energy, which will set the tone for your whole week.

Nothing affects personal and professional satisfaction like your energy level. There is no substitute for personal energy. Few things will affect your capacity for life more than your personal level of energy. Your ability to influence your energy level should not be taken lightly.

The Four Levels of Energy

In order to manage the level of energy in our own lives we need to understand not only the people, places, things, and activities that energize us or drain us of energy, but also the different levels that exist and the types of emotions that are related to each. There is literally not an aspect of life or business that is unaffected by the four levels of energy. Understanding them and approaching people, situations, and projects with the four levels of energy in mind can be immensely stimulating especially from a creative or innovative perspective.

To understand the four levels of energy on a very basic and intuitive level, consider this example. Sometimes you walk into a restaurant and as soon as you walk through the door you think to yourself, "I like this place!" You haven't tasted the food, you haven't seen the menu, and you haven't experienced the service—but on some level you have already decided. On another occasion you may walk into a restaurant for the first time to meet some friends for dinner and immediately think to yourself, "Why did I agree to let them choose the restaurant?" You don't like it. Why? Again, you haven't tasted the food, you haven't seen the menu, and you haven't experienced the service—but on some level you have already decided. Restaurants have energy, offices have energy, stores have energy, homes have energy, books have energy, clubs have energy, cars have energy, and products have energy. Every person, place, thing, and activity has energy. If you visit the concentration camp at Auschwitz, you will feel the energy of the place. Someone could take you there and not tell you where you were, show you nothing on the property that would give away what it was, and you would still have the sense that something was not quite right in the place. Even decades later, the people, place, things, and activities of Auschwitz have an energy that cannot be erased. They say if you move into a home where a horrific murder or rape has been committed, you can sense something about that home that never allows you to be perfectly at ease. At the other end of the spectrum, since the beginning of time, people of all religious and spiritual beliefs have held certain places to be sacred. Whether it is the sacred sites of the Australian Aborigines, Jews, Catholics, Hindus, Buddhists, or Muslims, these places tend to have a very calming energy.

Consider a visit to your local supermarket. The flow of traffic to the supermarket has a positive or negative energy. The parking lot has a certain type of energy, good or bad. The facade of the building has energy to it. The interior design and the flow of people through it have an energy. Where the displays and stock are set up has energy, and how much stock is on the shelves creates an energy. Walk down any aisle and you will notice that every single product has its very own energy, and some products have better energy than other products.

Things and places have certain levels or types of energy, but so do people and activities. Think about the people in various spheres of your life. There are no doubt some that energize you and some that drain your energy. Some that you cannot wait to spend time with and others you dread having to get together with. Instinctively and intuitively you know which category people place themselves in when it comes to energy, but are you acting upon it? Are you living your life in such a way as to manage the flow of energy? Are you proactively and intentionally managing the using and replenishing of energy in your life?

Finally, activities have energy. Think about all the things you do in a professional capacity. Some of these activities energize you and some drain you. The same is true when it comes to the vast array of activities that make up your personal life. Some are energizing and some are draining. I am not suggesting that you should stop doing all the things in your life that drain your energy. To be completely drained of energy from time to time is really good for us. What I am suggesting is that we can largely control the flow of energy in our lives and that many things in our lives serve little or no purpose and drain our energy unnecessarily.

People, places, things, and activities can energize us or drain us of our energy. If we want to live life at performance level with passion and purpose, if we want to live with overflowing energy and enthusiasm, we all need to take a very close look at how the people, places, things, and activities that make up our lives are affecting us from an energy perspective.

With that in mind, let's explore the four levels of energy and the various emotions related to each. This will further help us to recognize that at different times we all experience different levels of energy, and it will increase our understanding of the role energy plays in our quest for personal and professional satisfaction. After all, there is a correlation between how much energy a person has and the level of satisfaction that person is experiencing.

Here are the four levels of energy in ascending order, level one being the lowest (least desirable) and level four being the highest (most desirable).

The first level of energy could be described as low energy and usually places us in a destructive state. At this level we often feel depressed, exhausted, burned-out, defeated, and overwhelmed. We all experience the first level of energy from time to time, even the most highly functioning people. Of course, we never want to experience the first level of energy. What drives us into this level of energy? The answer is usually a combination of things. Life happens and we lack the energy reserves to buoy our energy levels through a difficult time. Another common scenario is that we just get into a rut. We give priority to urgent things that deplete our energy and diminish our satisfaction levels, and we ignore the life-giving habits that provide the necessary energy to thrive in the modern world. The important point to make is that level one is unavoidable to some extent. We are all going to experience it from time to time; it is the extent that we have some control over. How often we experience level one and how long we experience it are what we have tremendous influence over.

The second level of energy could be described as high-level negative energy and again usually places us in a destructive state.

At this level we often feel angry, fearful, anxious, defensive, and resentful. Like the first level of energy, we all experience this second level from time to time. We never want to, but it is part of the human experience. Some aspects of second-level energy are the result of occasional fatigue. For example, you have had a long day filled with minor frustrations or are operating on insufficient sleep, and your spouse or child does something that puts you over the edge. You are taken by anger and lose your temper. You find yourself in level two. Whatever happened to cause you to get there will have a huge impact on how long you stay there. Other aspects of level two energy arise from long-term dysfunction in our lives. It is not always the case, but fearful, anxious, and resentful components of level two often fall into this category. And, of course, any ongoing fatigue makes us especially susceptible to anger, fear, anxiety, and resentment.

The third level of energy could be described as restorative or reflective energy and places us in a positive state of contentment. At this level we feel mellow, serene, and content. If we actively think about these states, we tend to desire them, but they require real effort. Whereas levels one and two can be achieved with virtually no effort, intentionality and effort are prerequisites to creating and sustaining levels three and four types of energy. Third-level energy is often acquired through activities like yoga, meditation, or simply taking a long walk in a quiet place. Of course, the constant interruption to life and thought created by the flow of e-mail and phone calls from a smartphone makes a level three experience almost impossible. Unless we are willing to unplug from the world of technology, it is very unlikely we will experience level three energy, which is critical from a restorative perspective.

The fourth level of energy is the crown jewel of the energy hierarchy. It could be described as high-level positive energy, and it is the place from where we live our best lives and effortlessly celebrate the-best-version-of-ourselves. At the fourth level of energy we are confident, joyful, enthusiastic, and invigorated. Not surprisingly, the whole world yearns for level four energy. We want to be filled with fourth-level energy, but we also want to surround ourselves with people who have fourth-level energy. Why? It is contagious, attractive, life-giving. It should also come as no surprise that the people, places, things, and activities that have resounding fourth-level energy tend to succeed.

It is also interesting to note that the whole world is attracted to fourth-level energy. It is therefore not surprising that the most successful salespeople have fourth-level energy and the most successful product packaging has fourth-level energy.

Think about it. You get a call from a sales person who is depressed, exhausted, burned-out, defeated, and overwhelmed, and he invites you to lunch. Do you accept that invitation? I think not willingly. Conversely, people tend to buy things from salespeople with fourth-level energy that they don't even need. Why? They get carried away with being around the energy.

In the same way, when the best consumer products companies in the world come up with a new product, do you think their leaders sit down with the marketing and design people and say, "What we are looking for here is a package that is depressed, exhausted, burned-out, defeated, and overwhelmed. And an advertising campaign that is angry, fearful, anxious, defensive, and resentful." Of course not. In fact, you can walk down the supermarket aisle and pick off the products that got it right and the ones that didn't. All of the most successfully packaged products have fourth-level energy.

In the same way, the physical locations of different businesses have different levels of energy. What is the energy like where you work? Interestingly, even within the same company different locations can have massively different energy. There are some locations that everyone wants to work at and some that are treated like leper colonies.

Your office or cubicle has its own energy. What is it like? Your home has its own energy. So does your car, your things. Every person, place, thing, or activity in your life has energy that is either energizing or draining.

So, to recap, the four levels of energy are . . .

Level One: Depressed, exhausted, burned-out, defeated, and overwhelmed.

Level Two: Angry, fearful, anxious, defensive, and resentful.

Level Three: Mellow, serene, and content.

Level Four: Confident, joyful, enthusiastic, and invigorated.

And you have more control over the time you spend in each level than most people are willing to admit.

Everything Requires Energy

Now, with all this in mind, imagine the impact energy has on your personal and professional satisfaction. If PPS is something that you are ultimately responsible for creating for yourself, then your level of energy is of paramount importance in this quest. In fact, there might be nothing that has a greater influence on the level of PPS you experience than your personal energy level.

This claim might seem ludicrous, but let's consider it. Of course, it is easy to say that many things are more important to your satisfaction and more influential upon it than energy— but if you don't have energy, can you do those things? What kind of a spouse or partner will you be if you are constantly depressed, exhausted, burned-out, defeated, and overwhelmed? What type of an employee or manager will you be if you are always angry, fearful, anxious, defensive, and resentful? And isn't it more satisfying to be around someone with fourth-level energy than it is to be around someone drowning in levels one and two?

Your energy level has an enormous impact on your PPS.

So how can you increase your energy level? Truth is, you

probably don't need me to tell you. Take a piece of paper out right now, and write down seven ways you could increase your energy. The ways we can increase our energy levels are almost limitless. Take a walk. Drink half a gallon of water a day. Do something for twenty minutes every day that you love doing. Take a dream seriously. Pursue something you are really passionate about. Express your gratitude for someone in your life. Ensure you get adequate quality sleep.

The bottom line is that everything in life requires energy. You need energy to get out of bed in the morning, and everything in your day requires energy. Your personal finances require energy. Your relationships thrive on energy. Your health and well-being require energy. Your career needs energy to progress. Being a parent requires tremendous energy. You need energy for the things you love doing and the things you just have to do.

Do you have enough energy for the things you love doing?

Do you have enough energy to have a great marriage or relationship?

Do you have enough energy to be a fabulous parent?

Do you have enough energy to move beyond effectiveness into creativity and innovation?

Do you have enough energy for your work?

Do you have enough energy to manage other people with courage?

Do you have enough energy for your best ideas?

Living the life we really want to live, the life we can be passionate about, requires courage. But often we are too tired to live with courage. You see, fatigue makes cowards of us all. I see this in my marriage, in my parenting, in my managing of people. Especially in managing people. If there is one thing that modern managing is lacking in spades, it is managerial courage: the courage to outline your expectations, to regularly inspect what you expect, and to hold people accountable to excellence. The process can be outlined easily enough. Managers will agree how important it is to succeed. But few actually do it with any regularity. Why? It requires real energy to outline what you expect. It takes energy to inspect what you expect. It takes tons of energy to hold people accountable. It takes energy to coach people in the areas where they have fallen short. And all this is just the regular course of business. Now imagine a situation where someone has actually done something wrong or failed the team. Not something enormous but not something insignificant. It is here in the middle ground that mediocrity takes its grip on a team or organization. Most managers ignore such a transition, or they speak to it in a way that resolves the situation but does not confront the person responsible in any meaningful way. Why? Managerial courage requires energy, and most managers are tired all the time. They are just trying to survive. And fatigue makes cowards of us all.

Everything in life requires energy. No energy, no life. And that's why I began with the idea that your experience of life expands with the more energy you have. Now, I won't speak for you, but I am all about increasing my capacity for life. I love the idea of increasing my capacity to love my wife and children. I love the fact that I can increase my capacity for my work and the other hobbies I am passionate about.

Interestingly, if you make a real effort to increase your energy levels, you will notice what I call the energy effect on your life. You will win more business or projects. You will have more friends. Your colleagues will want your advice and input more often. Your clients and customers (internal and external) will enjoy working with you more. You will become more fun loving, and your spouse or partner will enjoy your company more. Your children will gravitate toward you and your ideas. Your friends and neighbors will want to know your secret.

The whole world yearns for energy and is attracted to the people, places, things, and activities that have that energy.

Batteries Included

I grew up in Australia with my parents and seven brothers. As you can imagine, Christmas morning was an interesting affair. We would all wake up ridiculously early, sit at the top of the stairs, and elect one brother to wake our parents up. That brother would be told to go back to bed, and we would wait twenty minutes and then elect another brother. Eventually our parents would get up, and we were then allowed to go downstairs and open our Christmas presents. With the eight of us opening gifts there was always wrapping paper flying everywhere.

Each year someone would get a gift that had a minuscule note on the box reading BATTERIES NOT INCLUDED, which my parents had failed to see. In those days—and it was not that long ago—nothing was open on Christmas Day, and so one of us had our prized gift but was not able to play with it.

Some people are like that. If you look closely, they come with a little sign that says BATTERIES NOT INCLUDED. Nobody wants to manage these people. Nobody wants these people on their team. Nobody wants these people as their spouse, neighbor, friend, or colleague. They suck all the energy out of everything.

Decide to be a "batteries included" person at work, in your marriage, in relation to your health and well-being, in your personal finances, and in any other area of life that is important to you. Start to influence the level of energy that you are experiencing and sharing with others, and your life will expand accordingly. More energy means more satisfaction. The more you are able to increase your energy level, the more you will increase the levels of personal and professional satisfaction you enjoy and can share with others.

5

Systems Drive Behaviors

apoleon once said, "Those who fail to plan can plan to fail." If this is true, and I believe it is, then we need to consider the implications of this idea on our business, to be sure, but also in our lives. Do you have a life plan? How much time do you spend planning different aspects of your life? Of course, many people react violently to this type of talk, defending their much-prized spontaneity. I am as much a fan of spontaneity as most, but not to the extent that it robs us of passion and purpose and drains satisfaction from our lives. We need a plan.

Now that I have made my case for pursuing a more satisfying life rather than trying to impose balance, what life have you imagined for yourself? Do you in fact want to live the life of the fisherman in the story that I used to open this book? Or are you more inclined toward a more satisfying version of the life you have already chosen and are living? Is your life in need of a complete overhaul or simply some small but meaningful adjustments? Either way, you need a plan, and the best plans are built on a system that will ensure the sustainability of the plan.

Systems drive behaviors. There are good systems and bad systems. If the system is not designed properly, it can drive the wrong types of behavior. Take for example the recent macroeconomic meltdown that was facilitated by the housing crisis in the United States. The very simplest explanation is that the system that drove housing in the boom was a bad system.

It was a bad system because the desired outcome had been defined in the wrong way. The system was set up based on a desired outcome of selling a lot of homes. The system should have been set up based on a desired outcome of people keeping the homes they bought. In this system, commissions were paid to mortgage brokers when the homes were sold. If the homes went into foreclosure, they did not have to pay the commissions back. So they didn't care if the people they were lending money to were a credit risk. Or perhaps they did care, but not nearly as much as they would have cared had they known they would have to pay back their commission, and perhaps also a fine, in the event the bank foreclosed. If the system had been set up that way, far fewer bad loans would have been made.

In designing a system you get to direct the way people (yourself or others) behave. A system allows you to influence what people care about. In the above housing example the system taught people to think only about sales. It should have taught them to think about the risk of foreclosures.

Now let's take a look at a legendary system. Every day McDonald's serves tens of millions of burgers to consumers all around the world. Can you and I make a better burger? Yes. Can we make ten million of those better burgers every day? No. McDonald's has a delivery system that has been studied and copied, it fathered the modern franchise movement, and it is the envy of many of its competitors and people in far-reaching industries. It's not the burger that sets McDonald's apart; it's the system.

The system allows McDonald's to drive results in tens of thousands of stores around the world every day, in many cases twenty-four hours a day. You need a system that will drive satisfaction in your life twenty-four hours a day, three hundred and sixty-five days a year. This chapter is about introducing that system to you and teaching you how to use it to drive powerful results in your own life.

If you want to live a more satisfying life, chances are you could sit down and identify what that more satisfying life would look like (desired outcome). Once you had this vision of what a more satisfying life looks like for you, you could also probably tell me what you need to do to bring that more satisfying life about (behaviors). The challenge for more people (and organizations) is consistently practicing those behaviors. This is the genius of a good system. Systems drive consistent behaviors. A good system is the connection between good behaviors and good outcomes. It is this gap that most people fail to consistently cross. People know what their desired outcome is, and people know what behaviors will bring that about. They are just inconsistent in practicing the behaviors that lead to the desired outcome. That's why we need systems.

Consider New Year's resolutions as an example. Millions of people annually resolve to follow a new workout regimen. Whether it is to work out every day or three times a week, most have failed and forgotten their resolution by the end of January. Why? They lack a plan, a system, and accountability. Great systems are made up of a plan, a process, and accountability. Now suppose your New Year's resolution is not just to work out every day, but to work out every day with your best friend—your chances of success just increased 60 percent. Why? You have a plan and you have accountability. Or suppose your resolution is to work out twice a week and you schedule a trainer to work with you at the same times every week. Your chances of success just increased again. Why? Your friend might not have the courage to hold you accountable. It's your trainer's job to hold you accountable.

The point is, whatever change we want to bring about in our lives requires a system.

The whole work-life balance disaster happened largely because nobody proposed a comprehensive system to help people create such balance in their lives. As a result, although people and companies had the best of intentions, we just threw some ideas and some tools at people and told them to work it out. We wouldn't approach our most important projects at work that way, so why do we approach the most important projects in our personal lives that way?

If we want to increase the level of personal and professional satisfaction that we experience in our lives, we need to approach it strategically. We are not going to just wake up one day and discover we have stumbled into a life of satisfaction. It is not just going to happen. We need to be intentional about it. With that in mind, I now offer you a process that can significantly increase the level of personal and professional satisfaction in your life. I have been using this model throughout its evolution for several years and have been amazed at the focus, clarity, and energy it delivers when I am faithful to it. I am also amazed at how random, distracted, unproductive, and unsatisfying my life can become when I am unfaithful to the process.

There are five facets to the process: (1) Assessment, (2) Priorities, (3) Core Habits, (4) Weekly Strategy Session, and (5) Quarterly Review. All of these are interconnected and play either a macro or micro role within the overall process. To neglect one is to tamper with the system, which always leads the system to break down.

From the test group who took our comprehensive satisfaction survey, those who were faithful to the process increased their satisfaction level by 24 percent over a three-month period. Those who began to use the process but abandoned one or all parts of it along the way still increased their satisfaction level (the result of being intentional, if not strategic), but only by 7 percent on average. So I encourage you to be faithful to the process in its entirety.

Finally, before we embark on the system itself, I want to encourage you to take a broader, longer view of your life. At work you get paid based on a variety of things: experience, ability to deliver results, industry knowledge, what the market will bear, education, and other factors. One thing that people never consider, but which affects their compensation more than most other things, is the period of time they deal with or are responsible for. What does that mean? Well, at McDonald's it is someone's job to get you through the drive-through in ninety seconds. That person makes minimum wage, perhaps $7 or $8 an hour. There is a manager on duty responsible for that eight-hour shift. That person makes $12–$15 an hour. There is a store manager responsible for delivering the quarterly results. That person makes $20 an hour. There is an area consultant responsible for the annual results for a cluster of stores. That person makes $35–$40 an hour. This continues all the way up through the organization to the CEO, who is responsible for working out what McDonald's will be doing twenty years from now. That person makes $20 million a year, plus—or roughly $10,000 an hour.

Responsibility Time Frame	Hourly Compensation
90 seconds	$7–$8
8 hours	$12–$15
3 months	$20
1 year	$35–$40
20 years	$10,000+

If you want to change the trajectory of your career, change the period of time you deal with and think about. If you want to change your life, change the period of time you think about.

So the first step is, don't be in too much of a hurry to create the ideal life you have imagined. Personal and professional satisfaction are built like a castle, one brick at a time. We tend to overestimate what we can do in a day and underestimate what we can do in a week. In the same way, we tend to overestimate what we can do in a year and underestimate what we can do in a decade.

Take the decade view. Give yourself a decade to build the life you have imagined for yourself, one that is rich and overflowing with personal and professional satisfaction. Until you take the decade view, until you begin to imagine and plan what you can do in a decade, you have not even begun to explore your potential.

The Personal and Professional Satisfaction System

1. Assessment

Every journey toward something is a journey away from something else, and sometimes it is just as important to know what you are journeying away from as it is to know what you are journeying toward. Pinpointing your dissatisfaction is critical to the process of increasing your satisfaction. You may think you know the cause of your dissatisfaction, but there may be things you have not considered.

If you take another look at the short-form assessment of twenty questions on pages 48–57, you will notice that the first ten questions relate to personal satisfaction while the second ten questions relate to professional satisfaction.

Take the assessment once every three months for the first year and then twice a year after that. You can do this online at FloydConsulting.com. The online version will generate a report for you each time you take it, which you can keep to track your progress.

Now, identify the questions where you selected *a* or *b*. These areas deserve your immediate attention. On parts #3 and #4 of this system, core habits and the weekly strategy session, you will have a chance to address these points of dissatisfaction in your life.

Once you have identified your *a* or *b* results, reflect on those questions one at a time.

For example, consider item 13 from the assessment, surrounding the topic of energy after work.

a. When I come home from work I am exhausted and cannot do anything meaningful.

b. When I come home from work I often feel tired and lethargic.

c. When I come home from work I usually have enough energy to do what I need to do.

d. Most of the time when I come home from work I feel energetic and enthusiastic.

e. I always have energy for the things I like to do when I come home from work.

The topic of the question is energy. Perhaps you selected *a* or *b* when you took the assessment in chapter 2. Now when you reflect upon the question, ask yourself, "What could I do to move my answer to *c* or *d*?" Think about all the things that affect your energy level—food, people, sleep, activities. You might make the following notes.

• Take at least a thirty-minute break at lunchtime.

• Drink less soda and more water throughout the day.

- Be more conscious of whether the foods I am eating are energizing me or draining my energy.

- Take three to five minutes at the beginning of the morning and afternoon to plan my work so that I don't get into an overwhelmed state or survival mode.

- Sit quietly in my car when I get home and breathe deeply for a minute or two before going into the house so that I can be intentional about my time with my family.

- Adopt a consistent workout routine.

This process allows us to pinpoint an element of our dissatisfaction and create a prescription to overcome it. In this case we have enormous control over the situation, but there are other situations where we may feel quite powerless. Take for example item 16 from the assessment.

a. My manager is not at all interested in me as a person.

b. My manager shows occasional interest in my life and career.

c. My manager has my interests at heart as long as they do not conflict with his or her interests or the company's.

d. My manager has my best interests at heart.

e. My manager goes out of his or her way to help me develop personally and professionally.

The topic of the question is the relationship with your manager. Perhaps you selected *a* or *b*. When you reflect upon the question "What could I do to move my answer to *c* or *d*?" perhaps you come to the conclusion that nothing is going to change your manager, and having a conversation with your manager would only worsen the situation. This is sadly a situation many people find themselves in.

Are you a completely helpless victim in this situation? No. And to think that you are is a mistake. In the short term you may not be able to increase your satisfaction in this area, but in the medium term you have much more control than you think. If it is driving deep dissatisfaction in your life, you should consider moving to another group within your company or leaving the company and taking a role elsewhere. Or you may decide to wait it out, hoping that he or she will move on to another role. You get to choose between the active and the passive response to your dissatisfaction. The point is, you get to decide. You can do something about it.

So consider it again: "What could I do to move my answer to *c* or *d* for this question?" Perhaps you make the following notes.

- Discuss my dissatisfaction with my manager. (This may not be a viable option in some cases.)

- Start exploring other job opportunities within the company.

- Put together a current résumé.

- Resolve that if I leave the company I will write to at least three people above my manager sharing with them how this manager affected my daily life and informing them that he or she was the reason I finally had to leave.

In the same way, go through this process for every question where you answered *a* or *b*. You do not need to take all the action steps that you identify immediately. Just write them down in one place. Perhaps you will focus on one question at a time, beginning with the questions that you have near complete control over and working toward the questions that require the cooperation of other people.

If you had no *a* or *b* results, then you should identify your *c* results and start to ask yourself what it would take to move them to *d* or *e* answers.

This first element of the Personal and Professional Satisfaction System is designed to provide a system of measurement. If you don't measure it consistently, you won't change it. Why do we measure so many things in our businesses? Because measuring is one of the simplest systems—and systems drive behavior.

2. Priorities

Once you have assessed where you are in the areas of personal and professional satisfaction it is important that you consider what matters most to you. Establishing priorities is critical to the process. Without a clear sense of what our priorities are, everything is important, which means nothing is important, and we become victims of the tyranny of the urgent. Identifying our priorities is indispensable if we are to enjoy sustained periods of satisfaction in our lives. The most satisfied people tend to have a clear sense of who they are and what is important to them.

It is also unlikely that you can just sit down and make a list of your priorities. And even if you can, it is important to go through some sort of process to firmly establish priorities. The process tends to give us confidence in the outcome. If you do not have confidence in the process, it is impossible to have confidence in the results of the process.

One of the most useful tools I have come across in my career as a business consultant is the priority exercise. I find myself constantly using it with clients, but I also use it internally with my team and just as often in my personal life. It was first introduced to me by T. D. Hughes, one of our senior consultants at Floyd, and is one of the simplest but most effective tools in my tool belt. Let me show you how it works. I think you will find it a useful tool to establish your priorities, but I am also confident you will find it a useful tool in many areas of your life and business.

Now let us consider your priorities. To begin, turn your mind back to Tom's story in chapter 3 and the priorities he had established for his life. He listed them as:

1. Faith

2. Marriage

3. Children

4. Health

5. Work

Of course, plenty of things weren't on his list: friends, social life, financial security, extended family, travel, hobbies, etc. The first step for you is to gather a list of potential priorities.

In one of my seminars a few weeks ago, one of the participants, Jim, identified the six categories below as potential priorities. They were not yet in any particular order. We encourage participants first to put together a list of as many important areas of their life as they can come up with. Then we ask them to narrow down their list of priorities to what they think are the five or six most important. We then employ the following priority exercise to help participants prioritize their list. This is how Jim's priority exercise took shape.

Jim's main priorities in no particular order were:

Health

Children

Work/Career

Social Life

Extended Family

Finances

In our session we placed them up on a whiteboard and then led Jim through the exercise, which consists of deciding which is more important between each of the options in the following way.

The first set of questions that make up the exercise involves choosing between Health (first on the list) and each other priority on the list. For example:

Which is more important to you? Health or Children? Health or Work/Career? Health or Social Life? Health or Extended Family? Health or Finances?

We placed a checkmark beside the priority Jim voted for in response to each question. He answered Health to every question except the first (Children). Therefore, one mark was placed beside Children and four marks beside Health.

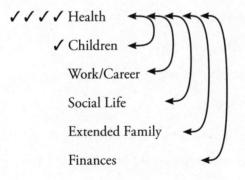

We then asked Jim to decide which is more important between Children (second on the list) and everything below Children on the list, one at a time.

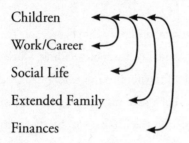

Children

Work/Career

Social Life

Extended Family

Finances

Which is more important to you? Children or Work/Career? Children or Social Life? Children or Extended Family? Children or Finances?

Jim chose Children in every case, so four more checkmarks were placed beside Children.

✓ ✓ ✓ ✓ Health

✓ ✓ ✓ ✓ ✓ Children

Work/Career

Social Life

Extended Family

Finances

Jim then had to choose between Work/Career (third on the list) and everything below that on the list, one at a time.

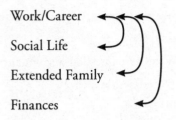

Work/Career

Social Life

Extended Family

Finances

Which is more important to you? Work/Career or Social Life? Work/Career or Extended Family? Work/Career or Finances?

Jim selected Work/Career in all three cases; so three marks were placed beside Work/Career. And so, you see the priorities beginning to emerge.

✓ ✓ ✓ ✓ Health

✓ ✓ ✓ ✓ ✓ Children

    ✓ ✓ ✓ Work/Career

       Social Life

       Extended Family

       Finances

Jim then chose between Social Life (fourth on the list) and everything below that on the list, one at a time.

Social Life

Extended Family

Finances

Which is more important to you? Social Life or Extended Family? Social Life or Finances?

Jim answered Social Life to the first question and Finances to the second. One mark was placed beside each.

✓ ✓ ✓ ✓ Health

✓ ✓ ✓ ✓ ✓ Children

✓ ✓ ✓ Work/Career

✓ Social Life

Extended Family

✓ Finances

Finally, Jim is asked, Which is more important to you? Extended Family or Finances? He answered Finances.

✓ ✓ ✓ ✓ Health

✓ ✓ ✓ ✓ ✓ Children

✓ ✓ ✓ Work/Career

✓ Social Life

Extended Family

✓ ✓ Finances

So, based on Jim's responses, Children has five marks, Health has four marks, Work/Career has three marks, Finances has two marks, Social Life has one mark, and Extended Family did not score at all. This, then, is Jim's priority list:

1. Children

2. Health

3. Work/Career

4. Finances

5. Social Life

Suppose for a moment that Finances and Social Life had both ended up with one mark. In what order would they then appear on the priority list? The answer is Finances and then Social Life. The reason is that when they were directly pitted against each other in the fourth round of the priority exercise (when he was deciding between Social Life and everything below it on the list), he selected Finances over Social Life.

Extended Family did not receive even a single mark, so while it may be important to Jim, it does not finish up on his priority list.

I asked Jim to share some of his reasoning and what his thoughts were now that he had quickly gone through the exercise in a crowded room in front of a bunch of strangers. He said that some things did not sit too well with him. Looking back he said he struggled deciding between the Health and Children priorities, because if he is not healthy he is no good to his children. He also observed that while the priority list was true to how he had been living his life, he saw that there needed to be some changes. For example, he spoke about how his wife had died four years earlier and at forty-six he still had a lifetime ahead of him and didn't want to spend the rest of his life alone. This caused him to observe that he needed to give more attention and perhaps priority to the social dimension of his life.

Your short list of priorities may be very different, and you may answer the very same questions Jim answered differently. Different things are important to different people. But I encourage you to take some time to do this exercise. Try not to rush it, and, at the same time, don't overthink it. Here is an outline of the process:

1. Make a list of all the many aspects of your life.

2. Reduce that list to about five or six of what you consider to be the most important aspects of your life.

3. Conduct the priority exercise on those five or six aspects of your life.

4. Take time in your weekly strategy session (#4) to review your priority list, especially when making decisions.

Visit FloydConsulting.com, where you will find a downloadable Priority Exercise worksheet for you and your team to use in establishing personal or professional priorities. If it is still unclear how the priority exercise works, you can also watch an instructional video.

It is helpful to come back once a year and reassess your priorities. At different times in our lives our priorities change either by choice or by circumstance.

3. Core Habits

Victor Hugo wrote, "He who every morning plans the transactions of the day and follows out that plan carries a thread that will guide him through the labyrinth of the most busy life. The orderly arrangement of his time is like a ray of light which darts itself through all his occupations. But where there is no plan, where the disposal of time is surrendered to the chance incidents, chaos will soon reign."

If you look back on the past ninety days, some days were better than others. There were probably some great days, a lot of fairly average days, and perhaps some bad days. What caused the great days? Was each one just happenstance, completely out of your control, nothing to do with you? Or are there certain things that you did that predisposed that day to being a great day?

Let's break it down a little further. How do your best days begin? When I ask this question in my seminars I get many different answers: working out; having breakfast with my children; taking some quiet time for prayer, reflection, planning; getting to bed early the night before; waking up rested;

giving myself enough time to get ready without rushing. The thing is, most people have never thought of it. It's a simple thing but true evidence of how little strategy there is to our lives.

You see, my own experience tells me this: if a day doesn't start as a great day, it is very, very, very unlikely to end as a great day. Once a day gets away from us, we tend to go into survival mode. Consciously or subconsciously we tend to start thinking to ourselves, "Alright, let's just get through this day!" Also, once a day gets away from you, it is very difficult to alter its momentum; it takes a lot of energy and attention to shift the energy of a day that has already gotten away from you. All this leads to the conclusion that it is best to take some time to set up a day. In doing so we give that day the best chance it has to be a great day.

Examining the best way to start your day is a great way to start living strategically. I did this for a long time, but then I started to examine my day on a deeper level. I started asking myself what components guaranteed (barring any disaster) that I would have a really good day. I came up with five things, and I call these core habits. Each year I reassess my core habits. Sometimes they change and sometimes they don't. But I know that if I do these five things on any given day the chances of me not having a really good day are pretty slim.

Core habits are the daily habits that keep you healthy, focused, and energized. Each year I choose a handful of core habits to ground my daily routines. These are my core habits for this year, in no particular order:

1. Forty-five-minute workout

2. Thirty minutes of meditation

3. One deliberate act of love toward my wife

4. Two thousand calories

5. One gallon of water

Let's walk through these one at a time.

Workout

I just feel better about myself on days when I work out. I have more energy and more focus. I cannot remember the last time I had a great day that did not include some sort of physical activity.

Meditation

My spirituality is important to me. It grounds me. It constantly holds my priorities before me and challenges me to grow. It allows me to find that quiet place deep within me and to live from that place. I am a-better-version-of-myself when I attend to my spiritual routine.

Acts of Love

I love my wife and I tell her that every day, but I think most of us have a tendency toward selfishness. So each day I deliberately make an effort to do one thing that I know she would like me to do (which in most cases I don't want to do) or something unexpected to demonstrate my love in practical ways. By looking to perform one deliberate act of love toward my wife each day, I end up doing many. Simply by opening our hearts and minds to this way of thinking, we begin to see opportunities for love all around us.

Calories

I love food. I love eating. This is a problem. There are many days when I am able to put away 4,000 calories without even trying, perhaps 5,000. But in truth, I don't need more than 2,000 calories a day. More important, I am most fully alive when I am limiting my intake of food to about 2,000 calories. A couple of years ago my doctor asked me to write down everything I ate every day and calculate the calories. He asked me to do this for a month. I was averaging over 3,500 calories a day. Extra calories suck the energy out of our days, and my best days require that I have self-control around food.

Water

Most people are dehydrated most of the time because of the lifestyles we follow, the food we eat, the beverages we drink, and other factors. Several years ago a friend of mine challenged me to drink a gallon of water every day for a week. It was a game changer. I had more energy, I ate less food, and I particularly noticed an increase in mental focus. In the same way, I challenge you to drink a quart of water for every fifty pounds of body weight every day for a week. It's harder than you think. Most days I fail to completely fulfill this core habit, but usually I come in between half a gallon and a full gallon. Hydrate yourself. It is critical to your health and success.

If I do these things, then it is a great day. It's not magic. No miracle is required. The list is specific, measurable, and realistic. There are many days when I don't do them all, and when that happens my personal and professional satisfaction takes a hit. Making it a great day means laying the foundation of these core habits.

Now it is your turn. Identify some core habits for yourself. Start with one. I began with one many years ago. It has taken me more than a decade to build up to five daily core habits. How do you get started? Ask yourself, "What would be a game changer for my days? What one thing, if done every day, would change my life markedly?"

Once you identify your first core habit, measure it. How many days a week do you do it? Perhaps it is four or five times the first week. Very well, beat that the next week. How many days do you do it the first month? Whatever the number, accept it as a challenge to do better the next month. But measuring it is critical. You will be amazed how hard it is to implement one life-changing daily habit. Visit FloydConsulting.com to download a series of measuring tools to help you succeed.

Once you are able to follow this habit about 80 percent of the time, add another core habit. Keep following the process until you get to the four or five things that ensure you have a really good day. Every year is made up of three hundred and sixty-five days just like today. Make it a great day.

4. Weekly Strategy Session

Without a strategy, failure in almost anything is inevitable. I am often amazed at how nonstrategically people approach their lives, even people who are well versed in the importance of strategy when it comes to business. In fact, only a tiny percentage of people approach any aspect of their lives with any strategy. For some it is limited to their personal finances. Others have a strategy for working out and staying healthy. But the person who has an overall strategic plan for their lives is very rare indeed. As I pointed out in *The Dream Manager*, most people spend more time planning their annual vacation than they spend planning their lives. Needless to say, as a result, most of us operate very inefficiently, often being pulled in the direction of the latest whim or loudest voice. Strategy and satisfaction go hand in hand. If we are going to experience high levels of personal and professional satisfaction, we need to pursue PPS strategically.

I have a friend who competes in triathlons. A triathlon is grueling by any measure. It is a multisport endurance event consisting of swimming, cycling, and running in immediate succession. A triathlon can involve various distances, but the Olympic distances are 1.5 kilometers of swimming, 40 kilometers of riding, and 10 kilometers of running. At the Ironman level these distances can increase to 3.8 kilometers of swimming, 180 kilometers of riding, and 42.2 kilometers of running. Each leg is a test unto itself. But interestingly the race is often won or lost in the transitions between legs. For this reason, the best triathletes plan and practice these transitions. On race day they set up their bike at the end of the swim and their running gear at the end of the bike route. This setup is called staging, and it is critical to victory.

Too often in life we do little or no staging. This staging is essentially planning for what is ahead, and it is a critical part of driving higher levels of PPS in our lives. A business without a strategic plan will not last long, and certainly it will not achieve anywhere near its potential. Our lives are also destined for underachievement and dissatisfaction if we don't learn to plan and strategize personally.

Myself, I have always been a planner. Too organized, some might say. But the tool I am going to lay before you now was introduced to me by a friend a few years ago and has been tremendously powerful in my life. The goal of this tool is to identify the key project that should have your attention and be your starting point for each day of the week. In the same way that our personal life needs a good start to the day, so does our professional life.

Too often I would come home from a full day in the office with the sense that I had done a lot of things but that I hadn't really done anything. A sense of accomplishment is essential to professional satisfaction. This tool is designed to create momentum for our days, from a professional perspective, and ensure that they don't get hijacked by e-mails and phone calls and meetings that mean little or nothing to our larger professional objectives.

Like the other aspects of the Personal and Professional Satisfaction System, the weekly strategy session is a very simple yet extremely powerful tool. Practical to its core, the system makes an impact that's impossible to miss even if applied for only a few days.

This is how I approach it. At some point over the weekend, usually Sunday afternoon, I slip away from the family for about twenty or thirty minutes to do my staging for the next week. The process is very simple. I identify the projects that I would like to move forward in the coming week. I often start by saying to myself, "If I do nothing else in the coming week, I will feel good about my professional life if I have moved these projects forward . . ." Then I list them. Most weeks I have five projects. I then look at my calendar, assess my other commitments, and allocate a key project to each day of the week. Sometimes I will have only three, and some of them or one of them will get more than one day. This week, I scheduled the whole week as a writing week to finish this book. So the same project is assigned to every day of the week. But to give you a sense of a regular week, this is what last week's strategy looked like:

Monday: Writing—*Off Balance*!

Tuesday: New Speaking Topics and Deliverables

Wednesday: Floyd Website Content

Thursday: Hollywood Casinos Proposal

Friday: Things to Do/Clean Up

When I first began to do this I noticed that my schedule was so full that I never got to these key projects, or that they got my worst time—the time when I was least efficient, focused, or creative. So I made one major change to the way I live my professional life. I stopped scheduling morning meetings, except to serve a client or when absolutely necessary.

Today, it is very rare that I will schedule an internal morning meeting. I may be with clients in the morning, but I don't schedule morning meetings in the office with my team. I start each day strategically, working on my focus project. Once I have moved that project forward significantly I move on to the busywork that every day involves. But now, because I have moved my key project forward, I have accomplished something. As a result, my psychological disposition to all the other work is completely different. If I don't do this, and certainly before I started doing this, too many days pass just filled to overflowing with busywork. Things that don't reflect what matters most kidnap my days—things that mean just about nothing, to just about nobody, and will mean even less to anyone a hundred years from now. In this way I find I am really able to add value to the business and to our clients, and I find there is a strong link between adding value and adding satisfaction.

If I don't have the discipline to adhere to this process, my days tend to end up at the mercy of everyone and everything else. Then the chances of my stumbling into the most important work are slim to none. So my life gets hijacked by the urgent things, which quickly diminish my energy for the most important things at work and the things I love doing personally. What does this type of day look like? In practical terms it looks like me sitting at the computer and responding and reacting to e-mails, sitting in meetings wondering whether I need to be in this meeting, and taking calls that completely lack strategic focus.

Each day has a focus, and holding to this focus plays a significant role in creating and sustaining high levels of satisfaction. I write my plans in a Word document and keep it on the desktop of my computer. I keep a printed copy on my desk at home and at work. Finally, I keep a copy in my wallet. It has my core habits on it and my weekly strategy.

You will notice that one day a week (in the above example it falls on Friday, but that is not always the case) I specifically and strategically allocate focus time to my "things to do" list. I also keep a running list of small and large things that need to be done in another document on my computer's desktop. I find that having a list on which to place these items and tasks frees my mind to forget about them until it is actually time to work on them. In the same way, having a time scheduled to do those things on the list liberates my mind from thinking about when I am going to get to them.

My father used to tell me that for every minute spent planning, twelve minutes is saved on average. That would mean that my thirty minutes on a Sunday afternoon spent planning, strategizing, and staging my week saves me six hours every week. I think my father was wrong. If I had to guess, I suspect that thirty minutes saves me ten to fifteen hours each week by helping me avoid wasting time and increasing my efficiency.

5. Quarterly Review

The most important part of any system is accountability. Without it most systems will fail, especially if they require that we use them consistently and voluntarily. When it comes to personal change or individual success, I have noticed that most people can do something for a few days, or a few weeks, but over time they tend to slip back into their old self-destructive ways. That's why we need coaches, managers, parents, leaders, role models, and mentors.

I am quite amused by the idea of self-directed work that is circulating at the moment in corporate America. In truth, most people are not capable of directing their own work. I don't mean that as a criticism of people, just as an observation of reality. A manager or company is not going to let people set their own working hours, decide what projects they do or don't work on, create their own budgets, etc. It would be lunacy—but that is self-directed work.

In the same way, self-directed excellence is not sustainable. People tend to achieve great things on their own for a relatively short period of time.

The final stage of the Personal and Professional Satisfaction System is all about accountability.

Now, I must admit that I am as allergic to accountability as most people. But it works. Once a week I go bike riding with my friend Nick. On riding days when the alarm goes off I never want to get out of bed. There has not been a single day when I woke up and said to myself, "I can't wait to get out there and ride today!" Not a single day. If he wasn't expecting me, if he wasn't going to be there waiting for me, if I was just planning to go riding on my own, most days I would probably just roll over and go back to sleep.

Accountability brings out the best in me.

In the business world we have the accountability of the annual review process. But annual reviews are not enough accountability to effect meaningful change because most managers don't inspect what they expect. To be honest, annual reviews are useless unless the results are managed throughout the year. Quarterly reviews are much more effective.

Forget about work for a moment. You need a quarterly review personally. This is the fifth and final stage of the system, and this is how it works.

Who? Spouse. Friend. Life coach. Someone who knows you enough to be able to speak to your life in a meaningful way. Someone who will quickly spot and call you on your excuses and justifications. Someone you feel sure has your best interests at heart.

What? Simply this: review what is not working well in your life; review what you said you would do in the last ninety days; outline the key objectives in your life at this time; share your plan to accomplish these objectives.

When? Once every three months.

Where? Someplace the two of you will not be interrupted, away from the distractions of daily life and business. Somewhere quiet enough to have the necessary discussions.

Why? To hold you accountable to the good things you want to do in your life and the person you want to be and become.

The system is simple. But it will drive powerful results in your life. It seems to me that people want to live deeply satisfying lives, personally and professionally. In truth, I think most managers and companies want their people to live deeply satisfying lives. But the reality is that there is very little companies and managers can do for us if we are not willing to take the quest for satisfaction seriously.

You can have a more satisfying life. You can have both personal and professional satisfaction. But nobody is going to just give it to you. It must be sought with relentless desire and commitment. Above all else, satisfaction must be sought patiently and with an overwhelming sense that we are responsible for creating satisfaction. While we can contribute to the satisfaction of others, nobody can be wholly responsible for our satisfaction other than ourselves. Does this scare you? I hope it does. If it does not, I fear you have skipped over the words without fully recognizing their truth. So let me say it this way. If you have a life filled with satisfaction, very good, you have given yourself this gift. If you have a life that lacks satisfaction, it is so, but only because you have chosen it. But you can choose again . . . beginning today, beginning now. Lillian Hellman wrote, "It's a sad day when you find out that it's not accident or time or fortune, but just yourself that kept things from you." I disagree. I think it is a happy day, as long as you are willing to do something about it. Are you willing to do something about the dissatisfaction in your life?

Epilogue

Satisfaction Trumps Balance

The fisherman has a great life—and so can you. In setting down these thoughts for you to read, my goal was to help you to think differently about your life. Have I succeeded? Only you can decide. It was also my hope to give you a system, simple and practical, should you want to do something about it now that you are thinking differently about your life.

Too often we think the life that we really want is unattainable. In some ways that may be true, but in other ways it is a complete myth. Imagine the life you want to live. It may seem impossible. But the tiniest slice of that life may be available to you right now. Grasp it. Enjoy it. Rejoice in it. Before you know it another slice of the life you have imagined will be available to you. Do the same. Grasp it. Enjoy it. Be grateful for it.

This is how lives are built. You don't sit down to a cake with a fork and just start eating. You cut yourself a slice of the cake, large or small, and sit down to enjoy it. In the same way, the lives we want to live are built one slice at a time. Stop waiting for the whole cake to present itself to you on a platter.

The discussion surrounding work-life balance has been mismanaged by companies and by individuals, but the bottom line is that people want to live more satisfying lives. They want more satisfying relationships and careers. In a recent Pew Research Center study only 27 percent of respondents were satisfied with their jobs. The Families and Work Institute reports that more than 50 percent of people feel overwhelmed by their work. A study conducted by Aon Consulting found that 88 percent of employees say they have a hard time juggling their personal and professional responsibilities.

The reality is that people are deeply dissatisfied personally and professionally. As individuals, we owe it to ourselves to do something about that. As companies, we owe it to our people to teach them how to implement systems in their lives that will drive increasing levels of satisfaction. Too often we don't know what we want, we approach our lives with no strategy, and in general we are hoping things will work out. It's time we took our destinies back into our own hands. We cannot sit around thinking, hoping, waiting for something wonderful to happen. We need to take a proactive approach.

And to the extent that we do, everyone who crosses our path will benefit.

Is life in the modern world a balancing act? Yes. What is the key to avoiding a fall? Knowing what really matters to you. For satisfaction does not arise from simply having experiences and things, but rather from having the experiences and things that you deem important. As we grow in wisdom we come to see that the things and experiences that help us become the-best-version-of-ourselves are the most valuable. It is with the onset of wisdom that we realize who we become is infinitely more important than what we do or have. In that wisdom we come finally to the realization that anyone or anything that does not help us become the-best-version-of-ourselves is just too small for us. We begin to see that many of the things we thought were so important hold no value at all. We also come to see what is of true importance. We arrive in a place of clarity.

Only then is a deep and permanent satisfaction possible. Because in the context of that wisdom so many of the voices that call to us each day fall away as insignificant and unimportant and we begin to listen, with primary attention, to that quiet gentle voice within us.

If we listen to that voice often enough and for long enough, and live by what we hear, we will arrive at a day when we can lay our heads on our pillows at night knowing that our lives make sense. Not that our lives make sense to others—our boss, our colleagues, the board, our family and friends, society, our community, or even our spouse. But, rather, that our lives make sense to ourselves.

To lay your head on your pillow at night, knowing that who you are and what you do makes sense ... now, that is satisfaction.

To learn more about the incredible work
Matthew Kelly and the Floyd Team are doing
to bring the ideas in this book to life
for individuals and companies—or if you would like
to explore having Matthew speak
at your next event, please contact:

Floyd Consulting

1235A North Clybourn, #109

Chicago, Illinois 60610

United States of America

Phone: 312-698-5025

E-mail: info@FloydConsulting.com

www.FloydConsulting.com